GP00122 9905

STRATEGIC REVITALIZATION

Managing the Challenges of Change
Second Edition

Douglas B. Gutknecht

UNIVERSITY
PRESS OF
AMERICA

Lanham • New York • London

Copyright © 1985, 1988 by,

University Press of America,® Inc.

4720 Boston Way
Lanham, MD 20706

3 Henrietta Street
London WC2E 8LU England

Printed in the United States of America

British Cataloging in Publication Information Available

First Edition published in 1985
Second Edition published in 1988

Library of Congress Cataloging-in-Publication Data

Gutknecht, Douglas B.
Strategic revitalization : managing the challenges of change /
Douglas B. Gutknecht.—2nd ed.
p. cm.
Bibliography: p.
Includes index.
1. Management. 2. Organizational behavior. 3. Organizational
change. I. Title.
HD31.G86   1988
658.4—dc 19   88–24839 CIP
ISBN 0–8191–7196–4 (alk. paper)
ISBN 0–8191–7197–2 (pbk. : alk. paper)

All University Press of America books are produced on acid-free paper.
The paper used in this publication meets the minimum requirements of
American National Standard for Information Sciences—Permanence of Paper
for Printed Library Materials, ANSI Z39.48–1984.

Dedicated to Cindy and Marleis, students in Chapman's Human Resources Management programs throughout the world, and all my friends and colleagues at Chapman college.

ACKNOWLEDGEMENTS

I would like to thank the following people for their ideas, assistance, support and encouragement. First, all my students and colleagues who gave support and assistance to this project: Bonnie Watkins, Pat Hetherman, Dave Gutknecht, Mike Price, Paul Erdmann and Jim Stream, and Joan Nogura.

Second, I would like to acknowledge once again, repeating my sentiments from the 1st edition of this book, Peter Drucker. During the the mid-1970's I taught at Pitzer College in the Claremont Colleges, and I had the great fortune to periodically attend classes and observe what a liberally educated, management teacher/thinker/philosopher could be like. Thank you Peter!

Third, I would like to acknowledge my colleagues in the Sociology department, the Human Resource Management Graduate program and friends throughout the Chapman community for all their support, intellectual stimulation, and commitment to making Chapman a quality-minded institution: Earl Babbie, Pat See, Karl Reitz, Roberta Lessor, Lee Estes, Jim Miller, Harry Schuler, Stan Califf, Howard Devine, Ken Tye, Barbara Tye, Jim Doti, Lynn Pierson Doti, Essi Adibi, Tom Beck, Don Booth, Barbara Mulch, and Ron Scott.

TABLE OF CONTENTS

PREFACE

This edition of **Strategic Revitalization** has over 90% new materal, and so can be viewed as essentially a new book. In fact, even the subtitle has changed from, **People, Processes, and Systems** to **Managing The Challenges of Change.** I will let you judge if the changes are substantial improvements or not. I have, however, tried to move the focus to a more readable and practical direction, to be of use to both academics and managers/administrators.

The nine chapters of the text explore various information, learning, and development strategies for proactively managing and mastering the challenges of change. Topics developed in some depth include the following: understanding and managing the challenges of change; using open-systems thinking and managing; the development of an active learning model to increase personal and organizational effectiveness; stimulating creativity for innovation; self-management strategies for behavioral change, increasing motivation, reaching goals, and learning actively over a lifetime; wellness and stress; organizational health promotion; the challenges of leadership; managing, corporate culture; and the uses of human resources management/development strategies for mastering the future challenges of change.

1

THE CHALLENGES OF CHANGE

INTRODUCTION

In times of rapid change, many organizational leaders are searching for more relevant and effective ways of accomplishing their work with a sense of quality, clear mission, and productive, long-term results.At the same time individuals are seeking increased responsibility, creative challenge, higher levels of performance and purpose in their work. Today, more than ever before, leaders, managers and employees are questioning how best to integrate their skills for enhancing the effectiveness of people, organizations, communities and world.

These commitments require of us all a renewed sense of purpose, vitality and energy to become more proactively involved. This search for revitalization and renewal will help us to set some parameters and know when we are on target and when we have missed the bulls eye. The process is aimed at educating our workers, organizations, and society about a renewed sense of purpose and what a more effective, productive and humane organization might look like.

This framework is built upon a linkage between three levels of wellness/health, effectiveness, productivity, purpose and performance: *the individual, group and the organization*. What is important here isusing this linkage when designing processes, relationships and systems for renewal.

We need to understand three key issues if we are to derive the benefits of linking these important dimensions. **First**, we can not continue to hold onto outworn patterns of behavior, like reacting to situations and problems after they hit and overwhelm our resources. **Second**, we are still relying upon a narrow set of assumptions to provide an adequate picture of the forces impacting our personal well-being and organizational productivity. **Third**, organizational leaders do not consistently act upon their stated visions, values, and beliefs. Leaders must show a more personal, living example, whenever possible, of their comittment to more humane, productive and open organizations.

THE HISTORICAL BACKGROUND

The machine or Mechanistic Age began during the Renaissance. The era signaled a total reawakening from the closed-eyed world of the Middle Ages. The ideas of scientific exploration, speculation, testing, uncertainty, curiosity and progress had been missing during much of the Middle Ages. Breaking down barriers to change, like disease, lack of movement and Medieval Catholicism, led to new ideas of enthusiasm, wonder and experimentation. These more exploratory and open attitudes replaced the closed, extra-worldly view of the Middle Ages (Ackoff, 1981: 6-8).

The Renaissance provided an opportunity for creative individuals to leave the university and find positions serving wealthy merchants or earning the patronage of princes. The birth of humanism stimulated an entrepreneurial outpouring as it elevated secular culture over the closed world of the medieval church and its more open world of the medieval university.

The emerging secularization of society revived the potency of the university to influence external events through the birth of modern science -- the synthesis of theoretical speculation with empirical observation and evidence. The important point for our purposes is not the history of science but the fact that social institutions and historical and economic forces influence theoretical and intellectual developments.

The question of why certain scientific and social ideas become successful during certain historical periods is often downplayed in favor of abstract ideas like objectivity and the sanctity of the scientific method. Knowledge, however, is not absolute or unchangeable; it is mediated by information, technology, social groups, institutional and organizational forces and national culture (Gutknecht, 1981, 1982). Social and institutional forces influence the methods, metaphors and world views of scientific and social thought at any given historical moment.

We observe these facts most acutely during the rise of the Industrial Age, which combined the scientific perspective with its emerging institutional applications to create improvements in manufacturing, expansion of commerce and increased funding for scientific research. The small yet emerging business and petty bourgeois were suppotting and being propelled by these trends.

The final driving force was the Industrial Revolution which began the process of replacing individual craft work and local village-based cottage industry with machine production processes. The result, first in England and latter in America, was the invention of mechanized, standardized, assembly-line production processes that were applied to manufacturing. Earlier products that resulted from this process, included farm implements, textiles and firearms; latter products included steam-driven water transportation, railroads, and eventually more consumer goods.

During this industrial era, the metaphor of machines provided a symbolic rationale for organizing work. Machines had a type of mystique and hidden logic that provided some explanation for the repetitive and routine reduction of material to more basic properties in organizations that operated like machines.

These machine products held potent images of wealth and dreams unfullfilled because cheaper goods slowly became available for consumption when produced on assembly lines, which reduced the unit cost of labor, materials and final products. However, fast production runs turned the assembly lines into endurance contests for many immigrant workers; while still providing the resources for savings, and the stimulus of upward mobility for a rapidly growing middle class.

Standardized tasks that employees repeated many times in a short span of time produced uniform job requirements that included little opportunity for ingenuity, innovation, the learning of new skills or the opportunity for understanding how one's work contributed to a greater final goal. The expressive metaphor of this period was, thus, mechanical or machine-like and contributed to a strong sense that freedom meant fighting machines and factories.

The mechanical metaphor influenced many aspects of organizational and social life in this industrial period: the perceived quicker pace of work, and even leisure activities; the perceptions of money or pay as somehow being less meaningful because it was less easy to link directly their work activity and rewards; the feeling that more socially-based needs were not now as important at work; the emerging spatial split betwen home as a place of family and leisure versus factory as a place of labor; the new distinctions between employer and employee; the rise of the powerful and sometimes autocratic bosses, whether company or union.

The mechanical metaphor and mechanistic world view underlies the emergence of large-scale organizations, scientific management theory (Taylor, 1911) and Weber's (1946) influential model of bureaucracy. The imagery of machinery predominated even here. Organizations performed routine, mechanized and standardized and centralized production work; later machine-like bureaucracies performed standardized supervision and management work. In either case skill requirements were low and training was perfunctory at best. By the 1930s, the entire production process had evolved to a state of standardization, meaninglessness, routine and inflexibility that Reich (1983) calls "technological maturity:"

> *As products evolved from low-volume, unstandardized, one-of-a-kind items, their associated production systems evolve from open and unstructured processes toward rigid and elaborately structured processes. In other words, a process*

product configuration or production unit that is initially fluid (relatively inefficient, flexible, and open to radical change) gradually tends over time to become stable (relatively efficient, inflexible, and open only to incremental change) (Abernathy, 1983: 17-18).

Industrial growth and market share soon depended upon the continued utilization of high volume and standardized production, which led to great increases in American capital for investment and increasing prosperity for more Americans. However, at some point in time these gains brought about by economies of scale, led mature industries to sacrifice their early legacy of entrepreneurship, technological innovation, and experimentation.

It is true that a decreasing rate of change in product technology reflects a shift in the basis of competition that rewards more efficient production. Standardization of design implies that, for any given product, the market has agreed that a certain set of design concepts best satisfies many perceived needs.

Along with this implication, however, comes another concern more detrimental to corporate long-term competitive survival: acquisition of competitive advantage through product innovation was not worth the investment in a safe or guaranteed marketplace. If the industry agrees upon an optimal set of design concepts, then there is no premium (in cost terms) for replacing one or more of them with innovative concepts made available through investment in additional research and development (Abernathy, et. al. 1983: 23).

Once cultural assumptions, processes, and structures were established, the job then became one of producing more of the most standardized products possible at the highest volume with the lowest unit cost. Technological applications to product improvements, however, soon slowed. Investments in new product design and improved technologies of production lessened; it did not fit a high volume manufacturing philosophy. Such incremental technical adaptation, rather than substantial, product betterment through innovation, became the norm, according to Reich (1983).

These industrial development strategies were not without initial reasons: they evolved over time to make profits and provide low-cost products, and a higher standard of living for everyone . However, markets do not remain immune from the forces of change, and competition does not stop because markets become dominated by mature and lazy industries. Some industrial giants, thus, living on their former legacy as innovators became overconfident and more vulnerable to their competitors. These innovative structures, and sophisticated technological processes would soon propel the competetion to the forefront of industrial and service leadership.

The problem today becomes how to renew Americam industry and move them away from mature or mechanical product and service strategies toward more proactive approaches. This framework includes many dimensions which are American management innovations.

STRATEGIC REVITALIZATION: WHAT IS THE PROACTIVE CHALLENGE?

The old reactive behavioral guidelines, policies, programs and models that describe how people and systems work are of less relevance today thanever before. These reactive approaches harbor assumptions that stifle the potential for innovation and creativity. And as Douglas McGregor (1960) taught us many years ago, managers and organizations always base their actions on implicit or latent theories and assumptions.

Organizational students, consultants and managers sometimes miss the essence of McGregor's view of the polarity in management styles because they fail to see that his terms are metaphorical and their usage reflects the tensions inherent in each of us as managers, leaders, and employees. McGregor was not writing a "how to" book for Theory Y managers or a book to lay blame only at Theory X style, but exploring how faulty assumptions often lead to ineffective leadership and management practices.   Theory Y only implies our potential to manage well, if we can become more self-aware and examine those narrow personal assumptions which support our ineffective management practices.

McGregor built his theories upon the research of Lewin, Maslow, and Herzberg which emphasized the following ideas: redesigning work systems to make quality everyone's business; making staff work as coaches not cops; iniatating the principles of effective teamwork; fitting people to jobs; giving workers more control over their own development; and emphasizing the importance of a system of management, not just technical mastery. However, he did place the burden of change upon each manager, and urged them to examine their own management assumptions (Gutknecht and Miller, 1986: 36-37; 110-115).

Each of us has probably found times in our lives when we were acting upon our own Theory X assumptions as a complement to our Theory Y assumptions. In addition, each component, Theory X or Theory Y, has both positive and negative aspects. If we wish to become effective leaders, managers, workers and individuals, we must accept our limitations, our very human nature, and always begin any assessment with our own values and perceptions of the situations at hand. This personal self-assessment and assumption analysis is essential for building both individual and organizational productivity, performance and healthy systems. We need to examine our faulty assumptions, while avoiding destructive win-lose thinking and dead-end self-fullfilling prophecies.

PROACTIVE AND REACTIVE ASSUMPTIONS

Whether conscious or not, many of these negative/reactive assumptions guide our expectations and eventually our behavior, reinforcing the results that we planted in our minds earlier in the cycle. This observation has many parallels in organizational thinking and practice. Managers who think workers are ignorant or lazy, will then act upon this assumption and get results like passive workers and shoddy, marginal work. Here are some additional harmful assumptions for all of us to think about:

* You don't need to respond to issues until they become major problems or someone in charge becomes aware that something is wrong--"if it's not broken, don't fix it."

* All problems can be broken down into logically arranged, component pieces and solved independent of each other, as long as we use rational and logical problem-solving methods.

* It's all right to blame our failures on other individuals and trends beyond our control. Let's think of ourselves as the property of those we work for and find an other way to shift responsibility.

* Let change dominate us and make sure to display surprise when someone tells us that the hand writing was on the wall all the time.

* Adopt a philosophy which views innovation as abrupt and drastic change in the normal mode of operations through large investments in new technology and equipment. This assumption is one of a giant leap forward and is geared toaccomplishing the big breakthrough, receiving immediate gains and instant recognition.

In contrast, proactive assumptions suggest more healthy and dynamic possibilities that are applicable at any level of personal behavior or system effectiveness:

* Anticipate issues and concerns before they become problems, erupt into crisis or overwhelm our abilities to respond effectively -- "attend to it constantly, even before it breaks down".

* All problems can't be reduced to logical pieces of a puzzle and solved independently of each other. Complement rational problem solving methods with creative and innovative thinking.

* Take responsibility for your own destiny, anticipate and examine behaviors, values and trends which might negatively impact you or your company in the future.

* Keep ahead of change by managing it--become a student of change. Don't let yourself ignore the signals which indicate that something is even slightly wrong, even when it appears to most people that everything is perfectly all right.

* Adopt a philosophy which views success, wellness and productive living as an integrated, and gradual process of improvement--practical outcomes that must slowly be built upon a solid, long-term foundation.

The signals are becoming clearer everyday that the old world is dramatically different and new assumptions and creative responses are now demanded. Today, a more comprehensive model is needed, one that includes concern with the most unique dimensions of the individual and a vision of system possibilities. This is why creativity is so important today. We need to understand what we are up against in the competitive marketplace, that we encounter locally, nationally, and internationally.

Conventional ideas about how organizations manage change, new workers, and competitive markets are under siege. More voices are being raised to challenge narrow and short-sighted organizational models and perspectives. The challenge ahead is that we involve our entire system in order to utilize our most innovative capabilities for constant learning and innovation.

New learning possibilities point the way to a more humane and productive future. Well-worn formalities provide no certainty under the onslaught of rapid change and competition. As an ongoing learning system we need more vitality, flexibility, and diversity to anticipate and prepare for even more rapid changes to come.

CHANGE: A PRIMER

The challenges of change are upon us; the volatility of changes in new technologies, information and international events are enough to make any leader or manager feel the dizzy exhilaration and sometimes apprehension over the rapidly changing local and global landscape. As Bucky Fuller reminded us several years ago, think globally and act or participate locally, but do them both together anyway because that is the future! Underlying all our interpretations of the meaning of change and transition in our lives is the fundamental need to--become involved, preserve our dignity and sense of purpose, and participate in deciding the direction of our own fate and future circumstance.

Change is the name of the game today. Our world can only rejoice because its deepest problems are not static. Everyone will become impacted by the nature and rate of change. No one will avoid the effects entirely. Many of us will have some say regarding how these changes will be implemented and will be able to emphasize how to capitalize on the positive effects and lessen the negative impacts. None of this will be simple: everyone, however is responsible for the results in our world.

Since we live in an age of rapid change, increasing international competition, new trends and fads, and an epidemic of mergers, cutbacks and takeovers, we need to know more about what impacts these events have upon our lives. This time of discontinuity, turbulence, and unpredictable change poses great challenges for individual wellness, personal careers, management education, and organization health and productivity. Organizational and management thinking-must become more innovative in a world where constant transformation is the standard, not the exception.

These facts call for more aware and information and knowledge rich organizations and personnel. Johnston (1986) persuasively documents the need and effectiveness of more liberally educated managers:

> *Briefly, we, too, are struck by the pervasiveness and increasing rapidity of change and the need for adaptability. But, we see in all this a strong case not so much for job-specific skills training as for educational breadth...But, largely because it fosters adaptability, we regard broad or liberal education as the best possible foundation for sustained management productivity.*

Since we live in an age of such rapid change and global competition, we need to learn more about the trends and events that impact our lives. Naisbitt (1982) has labeled some of these rapidly changing events mega-trends:

*The information society;
*An expanding emphasis on the humane and people centered aspects of technology;
*The global economy;
*An emerging long-term focus;
*Rapid decentralization of large scale and bureaucratic organizations;
*Increased emphasis on self-help;
*More participation by all levels of the organization in decision making;
*The rise of the network as a means of sharing information;
*Shifts in the centers of power and influence;
*Finally, an increase in the choices and options that eachindividual must face and master.

Although many will acknowledge the unique manner that Naisbitt has identified, organized and reported these trends through his content analysis and summary of vast amounts of already published trends, the approach itself is not that new. The true value of Naisbitt's work is the integrated perspective that it provides. Let's each try to identify some recent trends that demand our most vigorous and creative thinking.

MANAGING CHANGE : A GENERIC APPROACH

Change is something to which we must learn to adjust. How can we become more synchronized with its fluctuating demands, when we fail to incorporate its difficult realities into our organizational visions, values and business plans? The practical impacts of change are knocking many businesses out of the international competitive game because they have not recognized and developed a practical strategy for incorporating changes beneficial aspects. We must learn to read the signs of change and thus, make change something we both understand and can utilize.

The key is to recognize that change is continuous, indeterminate and incoherent. It is impossible to precisely predict or easily adjust to it. Change is now such a riddle because we try to hard to think in old terminology and categories. What we really need to do is become more proactive in our general thinking and try to manage, not master change. This strategy is practical and focuses upon the nature and impacts of change wherever we find them.

LEVELS OF REACTION AND RESPONSE TO CHANGE

When faced with the realities of unpredictable and chaotic events, we often rely upon one of several strategies. First, we can ignore or deny the realities of what is happening around us. Second, we might reactively adjust to changes after the impacts have devastated our ability to adequately cope Third, we can profitably anticipate some of the negative impacts and focus upon using our knowledge of the positive dimensions of change to devise practical strategies to profit from change. The goal of managers is to move as quickly as possible from denial to the utilization of change management as a business strategy.

Every leader and manager must find time to think about the sign-posts of change. By understanding the trends indicating changes that lie ahead, leaders, managers and human resource professionals can capitalize on the ignorance of their competitors. They must also approach the topic with both creativity and humility by recognizing their limits to easily exploit change. Organizations must design this awareness process into their business planning, work culture, organizational structures, training and human resource reward systems.

Each persons perception of change can occur on many different levels and involve many stages of understanding. However, understanding seems to become more abstract the deeper it becomes. What is needed is a practical view of change that is compatible with our emphasis on renewal and results, not just abstract inquiry. This **action data** focus must become part of our work culture.

CHANGE PRINCIPLES

Let's explore some research on change that will indicate several principles helping us to take advantage of positive change opportunities. We must always recognize that changes take place within a time-bound world; it will not be an effective change unless we consider the issue of timing. We often satisfice rather than optimize because of the constraints of time and the impossibility of deciding the best alternative. And time itself is only meaningful when we measure it through changes: the before and after pictures of changing impacts.

Change is always meaningful because it is **subjectively determined and felt.** People perceive the impacts of change in their own emotional way. This ability is limited by our fears, low self-esteem, lack of education, inability to distinguish good from bad information, and our failure to understand the perversity of human nature. Thus, we need to understand the human dimensions of change. We must learn more about how people emotionally interpret proposed changes to determine whether they will embrace them or resist them. To do this, managers must begin by becoming more empathetic toward their workers when changes are proposed.

Kirkpatrick (1988:1212-117) suggests that three things are needed for making change more effective. **Empathy,** along with good **communication,** and **participation are the three keys** to successful change. The way to become empathetic is to learn more about your employees, and also try to understand some of the barriers that will prevent leaders and managers from reaching rapport with employees: being preoccupied with something more important; not interested in the message; don't respect the sender; think you know what the message will be before it is sent; don't want to understand; being physically tired; thinking about other things than the message; being distracted; pretending to listen or understand.

Change is often difficult to categorize and measure because it defies any complex modeling of cause and effect. Change is often seen as both cause and effect ;separating them isn't easy. Change effects are often not perceived immediately because the time lag between the initiation of change (cause) and perception of impacts (feeling or seeing) the effects. When we squeeze a variable (event or action) and the expected effect is delayed, we are feeling the impact of this time lag.

By **appreciating the limits** (not the need to eliminate) of traditional methodologies for managing change, we can **supplement our usage** of this type of research with additional approaches. Some of the problems that arise using traditional methodologies to study change are as follows: ignoring cumulative effects such as tolerance thresholds, which when reached no longer yield the same effects (how high can we raise tuition based upon an additive model); the inability to predict how people will respond to change; that change is seldom linear and thus change often accelerates or diminishes because of physical limits or interactive effects (some modeling techniques can explain adequately some of this variance in more stable fields); how to quantify intangibles, like intuition, timing and creativity; and finally, the fact that our observations of certain social phenomena actually alter them.

Let's be clear on this issue: the traditional scientific method does have an important place in the academic arsenal of tools and techniques for improving our understanding of how organizations can profitably and effectively work. These techniques work most effectively when coupled with good business planning and when the timing of change is not immediate issues. However, good leaders and managers often need to quickly discover the essence of complex relationships, trends and conflicts in order to respond immediately to emergent and unanticipated issues.

We need to trust the experience and gut feelings of effective leaders and managers with a good track record. This type of experience is not unscientific just because it often builds upon the creative and uniquely systematic ways that leaders focus on important trends and issues. Just try to quantify timing. Yet, it is relatively easy to find effective executives who have used the lessons of experience to become masters of timing, outwitting change more often than expected.

Change is value-based because it impacts and even expresses our most important priorities. It is very hard to quantify value precisely because it depends upon perception and other experiential skills, including maturity, length of time at the job, and degree of responsibility working at numerous aspects of the business. The nature of change provides **data for use** as we improve its beneficial dimensions and reduce some of its negative effects.

Waterman (1988) has recently used the terms , "friendly facts" and "congenial controls" because he wants leaders and managers to make the distinction between neutral data and valuable information. The latter should set parameters for more effective strategies and actions. Traditional control strategies are based upon outdated, unprioritized data that feedback irrelevant or garbage signals (reactive use); while modern control strategies prioritize and organize meaningful data (information) to allow us to anticipate change trends and and feedforward opportunities (proactive usage).

Some of his **action suggestions** include: cutting costs without lowering quality (need priorities and good facts); using a common fact base for communication about direction and results; treating financial controls as liberating; pushing for better cost information; insisting on comparisons of information--differences from expectations, historical experience, competitors in same industry, and customer needs; finally, becoming friendly with computer spreadsheets because they provide opportunities to make comparisons (Waterman, 1988:132-135).

Let's explore some additional features of change. We must more astutely use the power of change expectations and anticipation. Before change can be profitable, people must know about it ; this will also reduce resistance. We are limited by our fear of change and other barriers; the same barriers that constrain our creativity (see chapter 4). Managing change requires us to remove these barriers. We must also learn not just to measure i,t but sense it and touch it in our gut. Good leaders know the value of hunches, seat-of-the-pants experience, and timing.

Some additional features of change that we need to learn more about are discussed below. Change data are often transformed and lose distinctive characteristics as they move up the information pipeline; we must lessen this line loss in order to derive any value from change information and reduce information costs. Insensitive management communication styles also lead to either over or under inflated assessments of the value of change information; this causes information to worry and shock us.

At some some point in time we must stop trying to simplify change and begin to use it to our advantage. What we really need to do is recognize that change is complex; so our models must try to focus on specific areas that make a difference: that balance simplicity with cost, accuracy and benefits. We must empathize, communicate and empower our employees because they are the ones who see and respond to change; yet, they often don't have the power to act. When we try to use old models that optimize reactive viewpoints for the short-run, we focus to narrowly upon variables which ignore the major influences just beyond the reach of our methods.

Liberally educated leaders and manager generalists know how to move beyond a narrow focus, with expanded information outside our traditional areas of concern. Because we all sometimes suffer from information overload and a limited threshold for tolerating things unique or different, we then reduce the number of things that we pay attention to. The value of any well designed information system is that it can provide us with the relevant information that we need to manage change and face the competitive challenges ahead.

The following **action strategies** and some companies that missed or made the mark are derived from Peter Drucker and will give us an opportunity to reflect upon some things that we might do to manage change in a more entrepreneurial way.

    1. Look toward the **unexpected**--success, failure, or outside event (Nordstrom's unexpected success with it's customer service strategy, new small specialized steel companies/unexpected failures of Nisssan cars)

2. Examine incongruities--between what something is and what it ought to be (between costs of health care and increasing need for it on the part of the elderly).

3. Explore innovation based upon **process need**--perfect a process that already exists, replaces a weak link, redesign an old existing process around new knowledge (national newspaper U.S.A. Today, new private schools for reading skills, company devoted to home health care products).

4. Probe industry or market structure--autos in 1970's; in the late1950's firm of Donaldson, Lufkin and Jenrette which focused upon a whole new generation of customers, the pension fund administrator; MCI and Sprint during the breakup of A.T.T.; medicine today; big American producers of aspirin could not see the value of "non-aspirin aspirin" until new companies had a market foothold; the post office resisted innovation many years until U.P.S. and Federal Express exerted their competitive muscle).

5. Examine changing demographics, moods and **perceptions** in society and **new knowledge**--(baby boomers, elderly, women in the workplace, more educated workers, yuppies and affluent lifestyles, convenience foods for busy families.

CHANGE MASTERS

Kanter (1983) has identified the following seven key elements as characteristics of what she calls "change masters".

1. Tuning into the environment--being aware of emerging trends and new ideas that effect the competitiveness of the company in the marketplace.

2. Kaleidoscope thinking--perceiving new and more creative possibilities in old ideas.

3. Communicating a Clear vision--having the ability to inspire others and get them excited about your vision.

4. Building coalitions--recruiting supporters and resources to get your vision accomplished.

5. Working through teams--achieving commitment from important people, possible supporters and others who are important for moving ideas into action and completion.

6. Persisting and persevering--Working through blockages with flexibility.

7. Making everyone a hero--trying to get credit for everyone involved in a project.

DEMING'S 14 POINTS FOR MANAGING CHANGE AND QUALITY

Another useful model for mastering change and achieving quality products and services is a model developed by Deming (1988). In fact, Deming is the key person portrayed as being responsible for the transformation of Japanese business after WWII.

1. Create a constancy of purpose for product or service improvement], assign quality responsibilities and hold people accountable.

2. Adopt a quality philosophy of zero defects because we can no longer live with the traditional standards of acceptable levels for delays, mistakes, defective materials, or workmanship.

3. Don't rely upon mass inspection or end of process measures as evidence of quality. Build statistical inspection into the work process in the first place.

4. Don't award business on the basis of the price tag, but do award on the statistical evidence of quality. Minimize instead, total costs and move toward a single, quality orientated supplier for each item. Build a long-term relationship with suppliers.

5. Management must continually work upon improving the organization's systems through continuous evaluation of work design.

6. Institute a modern on-the-job training system.

7. Change the focus of supervisors from large span of control to concern with quality. Productivity will automatically increase.

8. Drive out fear so that everyone can work more effectively

9. Break down the barriers between departments.

10. Eliminate slogans and targets, ask for increased productivity without providing proven research and methods for productivity improvement.

11. Eliminate work standards that prescribe numerical quotas.

12. Remove barriers that prevent pride of workmanship for hourly workers.

13. Institute a vigorous program for education and self-improvement in your organization.

14. Put everyone in the company to work to accomplish the transformation of the organization. Make this transformation everybodie's job and give everyone the tools to become more aware of the process requirements.

FACING THE COMPLEXITY AHEAD

Many trends in our society, organizations and personal lives can be understood and anticipated. However, we must also transcend the fads and fashion which destine us to grasp at out-dated ideas. We must not waste time, energy and resources. Signs of lost opportunities and fears of the future require ongoing personal and organizational planning, thinking and learning--strategic revitalization.

Surprise itself, which should motivate us to at least question where we are going, immobilizes us because we often cannot respond to what we don't expect. Expectations escalate as we fail to understand the modern worker--their potentialities, interest, needs and values. We must learn to focus upon energizing common values through imaging scenarios of future possibilities, not just lists of problems.

Organizations must learn to maintain an active and participatory environment. Yet unfocused motion and activity can't teach us to strategically select those tasks worth doing. When we fail to learn how to effectively plan our future, we lose patience, follow the whims of trend setters and lose our sense of direction and purpose. Piecemeal and passive planning produces a negative and defensive person or organization. We soon feel overwhelmed by the complexity before us; uncertainty blocks our every move.

Complexity creates great personal and organizational uncertainty and stress. We become overwhelmed by stimuli and information, and fail to make sense of changing trends. We also ignore the importance of perspectives for interpreting trends and events around us. Complex problems hit us hardest when we are unprepared to anticipate and plan for constant change, as opportunities for renewal.

The issue is one of setting our priorities and establishing a systematic framework for supporting compassionate interdisciplinary and systems thinking. Our difficulties, pains, problems and failures can become opportunities for cultural change, and organizational innovation. Tannenbaum and Hanna (1985) suggest that we cannot change organizations without expecting the human need to hold onto certainty and some control. Ferguson (1980:32) inspires us to push outward and enlarge our vision by allowing new assumptions, behaviors and perspectives to emerge:

> *The gift of insight--of making imaginative new connections - once the speciality of a lucky few, is there for anyone willing to persist, experiment and explore.*

Both individuals and organizations must find the will and the means to use new information, technologies and education/training to anticipate, guide, encourage, motivate, empower, clarify, elaborate and assist in bridging the gap to new innovations, strategies. institutions and perspectives. Crozier and Friedberg (1980:15) offer this insight:

> *People are not made freer by getting rid of organization but by developing it. Management doesn't necessarily mean authority, but always requires voluntary action and conscious involvement.*

The nature of modern complex systems and problems creates much uncertainty in our individual, group, organizational and national lives. We need innovative strategies, systems, processes, tools and behaviors to ensure our survival and to encourage the building of truly Democratic and authentic work communities. This long-term view of the need to preserve democratic possibilities will enable us to put people to good use and work through expanded employment brought by competitive organizations which can increase economic stability and opportunity for us all.

However, both individuals and organizations often seem incapable of changing their directions and taking the long-term viewpoint. Instead, they fall back upon blaming old strategies and convenient scapegoats; failing to accept blame they try to cover their errors. Leadership in such a situation is sorely lacking.

Uncertainty, like conflict, is seldom solved in any optimal or final way, although it can be managed and reduced. They key to reducing the negative consequences of uncertainty is to build system linkages that allow us to acknowledge interdependence, to value feedback, to support new forms of experimentation, and entrepreneurial risk taking. We must continue the search for ways of effectively building upon self-interest, in order to strategically expand those behaviors, support structures and cultural values that foster productive collaboration and teamwork for innovation at all organizational levels.

RECOGNIZING HOLISTIC AND LONG-TERM ASSUMPTIONS

Today, we live in a world of complex and uncertain situations, which don't produce simple problems that can be easily diagnosed and solved. Many managers and leaders still, however, act as if the world were simple. The outcomes produced bysuch an approach to change can be quite destructive to organizational survival.

Those responsible for effective and productive organizational problem solving and decision making can discover that it is in their best interests to support strategies that promote innovative, long-term thinking and learning. However, many still plead ignorance of these assumptions by following so called traditional practices which support personal privilege, status, or routine (business as usual). Such actions continue to perpetuate conceptual blindspots (Weick, 1979; Frost, 1984) and a strategy of crisis management.

Many individuals in organizations waste energy and preserve their ignorance by supporting reactive assumptions because change is often difficult to face, even for the most flexible individuals. It is easier to blame others and avoid responsibility. The preservation of ignorance is often taught to subordinates and passed along to associates because it allows everyone to avoid the turmoil and costs of change, even if such changes will possibly create an environment that will spawn more effective and creative organizations.

Too often, organizational leaders and workers learn techniques to ignore valid, useful, creative and innovative information, which could enlarge their competence to manage the destructive effects of change. All organizational members can become more alert to the possibilities for creating a more authentic and productive worker community.

One subtle and tell-tale sign of this attitude is a fear of conflict and change. The situation occurs most often when individuals and organizations reject valid and useful information for self-serving reasons and personal gain. Distorted and error-filled feedback produces a stulifying status-quo, which supports an abnormal fear of change. The build-up of routine and conservative patterns then leads to habits which blocks more basic learning. Such habits include avoiding the examination of important values and assumptions. Fear of change, innovation and creativity is the result.

Organizations in turbulent and competitive environments seem particularly vulnerable to failure, if they follow the path of change resistance. Organizations develop numerous strategies for narrowing the field of appropriate feedback, because exposure to information may reveal unfounded professional status, prerogatives, and claims to privilege. Enlarging the organizational frame of reference about assumptions and values (its culture and leadership) can call attention to such protective and selfish behaviors.

Many organizations unconsciously teach their workers to win and lose at the expense of others. This preparation for obsolescence will continue indefinitely unless alternatives are proposed by enlightened leaders. Mangers soon become accustomed to a fear of change and, thus, do not raise the appropriate questions. By learning to ask tough questions and gathering relevant information these narrow personal survival strategies appropriate in a sick or neurotic environment can be identified and eliminated. After all, why should we feel the pain of change when we can avoid it--who needs all the aggravation when pain avoidance is so easy and satisfying?

As long as we are not suffering today, expressing anxiety or losing power struggles, why can't we just continue those destructive and divisive games which inflate our egos, and continue our lucrative, yet destructive routines. Why should we feel responsible for risking our position in the organization, when things look satisfactory in the short-run?

Often, the problem is compounded because individuals are ignorant of their destructive behaviors; they lack self-insight or operate from a narrow set of assumptions regarding the tasks of effective leaders and managers. This inevitably harms both individuals and the organization.

In many organizations, a closed-system mentality often prevails and feeds upon itself. People learn to "freeze" into dysfunctional patterns in order to survive and protect their status, titles, and turf. Novel, innovative ideas are suppressed because they lack the right sponsorship or potential to elevate their bosses' private agendas. Leaders and employees run scared because they won't admit errors and allow others to question their ideas. Dialogue diminishes, feedback stops.

The culture of these organization often supports "segmentalist" or narrow values (Kanter: 1983). This encourages fear of change by rewarding aggressiveness and self-centered behavior. In contrast, participative management and a sense of group involvement and shared ownership can contribute to win-win situations.

Here the possibility of communicating a long range organizational direction is lost. So is the patience, perspective and commitment that come from a shared sense of involvement and ownership. By ignoring productive dialogue, interaction, feedback or system-wide cooperation, the mentality of "us" and "them" is fostered. Creativity and ongoing learning for organizational innovation can only occur through interchanges across numerous environments, enclaves and functions (Kanter, 1983). Insulation leads to "group think": (Janis,

1982), and the illusion of invincibility.

Organizations must learn how to accept the uncertainty that accompanies the changing world around us. Managers must acknowledge and pay attention to how their training makes them believe that leadership means having all the answers. They must acknowledge they don't have all the answers and find ways of using their intuition, experience and managerial skills to delegate and involve others in the problem identification and solving process. Many managers, leaders and professionals routinely face and adequately cope with daily complex decision problems (Schon, 1983). They build upon their experience to create a personal sense of competence and professionalism as they become part of an organizational culture committed to sustaining innovation and excellence.

THE NEED FOR STRATEGIC REVITALIZATION

The modern organizational system is part of a complex system, and understanding this fact allows us to move beyond single, narrow theoretical frames of analysis.   Understanding organizations today requires that we utilize multiple vantage points, depending upon the types or level of issues addressed.   To be locked into any one perspective, produces narrow self-fulfilling prophecies and fails to capture the complexity of rapid social change.   Today, we must emphasize a framework of multiple options and possibilities.

The perspective offers a certain set of assumptions, techniques, and visions of the possibility of expanding our understanding of modern organization.   In addition, it allows us to better see how our own lives and knowledge can be utilized to revitalize and enrich others. Each of us builds personal models of how our organizational and personal worlds fit together.

Studying organizations in turbulent and uncertain times as we move toward the 21st century requires new energy, enthusiasm, hope, wisdom and willpower to implement a more humane vision.   It requires us to see both the crises and opportunities ahead. We must improve perception of our organizations and institutions in order to see how our actions perpetuate and create problems; yet, also, we must provide the opportunities for exercising our human ingenuity.

We must not waste our energy by emphasizing insignificant and trivial matters. We must select our targets, identify where the action is, and move with creativity and resourcefulness. Old solutions and thinking are not enough. We can't afford the luxury of despair or blind optimism. We need new perceptions and understanding of how organizations can be structured to create optimal productivity.

Strategic revitalization is a way of conceptualizing, perceiving and thinking about the relationships of healthy organizations and and people. It is a way to systematically analyze, understand, and promote the ongoing vitality in organizational systems, processes and people.

This specific model for understanding organizational relationships and structures is used to see problems, describe patterns, help us design and structure organizations to better fulfill their purpose. Our task in improving the quality of work life should include a commitment to these assumptions:

1) A job worth doing: one that is meaningful and draws upon one's talents, skills, and knowledge to contribute to the short-term and ultimately long-term goals of the organization;

2) Advancement based upon merit and performance;

3) Feedback and recognition of both one's strengths and weakness, on both an immediate and periodic basis;

4) Opportunities, such as skills training, career upgrading and advancement;

5) Safe and adequate work environments,

including a positive physical, psychological
and social work climate; and

6) Adequate and fair treatment in advancement,
supervision, job description and job security.

New trends and shifts in values demand that organizations understand the importance of human resources. Human resource strategies must support the transition to a post-industrial world. Such strategies will become the catalyst for facilitating new work and organizational values. Such new values will themselves serve to provide road-guides and institutional support structures.

Many traditional work values, which once brought us success, will be modified. We still appear wedded, in many instances, to those values of control, top-down authority and classical management theories of decision making, worker motivation and productivity. In simple terms, we still measure, prod and quantify people and jobs as if productivity in the modern organization depended solely on reigning in employee energy and talents.

The conflict between the new and traditional work values has brought new challenges to the work place. The baby boom generation of workers are now moving up the career ladder. This bulge accounts for about half the current labor supply.

The issue for human resources development in the 1990's and beyond is how to accommodate the higher career aspiration of such a large number of valuable workers. Such workers have great expectations of contributing and being advanced as a reward. The inevitable mid-career bottlenecks of this group will cause new forms of discontent, conflict and competition. This harmful to individuals, organizations, and society. By 1990 the 25 to 44 year old cohort will experience much middle management upheaval because of the diminishing number of available middle level positions.

A baby bust, with lowered birth rates since the mid-sixties, means that the number of entry level workers in the 1990's will decrease.

Numerous implications include potential generational conflicts between highly educated workers, stuck with stagnant jobs, incomes, and diminished opportunity for advancement, and entry level workers, who will find wages increasing and qualifications lowered due to market conditions.

This scenario poses enormous potential opportunities and dangers for those committed to understanding and developing our most precious, organizational resource--people. Some organizations will adopt the short-term option of exploiting a much larger pool of mid-level talent, at the expense of long range resentments. Many organizational members will vote with their feet and exit; other will stay and become dead-wood or problem employees (Odiorne, 1984) as they experience unfulfilled expectations. Still others will rebel, organize, and give voice to their concerns by disrupting work life. The issues of enlarging the voice of workers, increasing motivation, opportunity, building loyalty, morale and quality of work life (QWL) become major challenges for the decades of the 1980's and beyond (Kerr, 1979; Abernathy, 1983).

Early industrial successes promoted the value of commitment to hard work. One's attachment to a job was instrumental, a means to an end, and not an end in itself. We now strongly support values like privacy, autonomy and self-direction. Modern workers demand more autonomy and choices regarding work relations and lifestyle choices outside of work. In addition, workers at all levels act freer with their superiors, and discipline is less exacting and onerous.

Some organizations concerned about the abdication of legitimate authority and leadership are attempting to aide workers, both inside and outside the work environment, with employee assistance programs--like health, wellness, nutrition, exercise, drug and family counseling (Pelletier, 1984). However, the work ethic (belief in the importance of working hard and quality work) has not declined significantly over the past thirty years. What has declined is the confidence the individual worker has in the ability of management to recognize the new worker, and their desire for high-quality involvement, mutual respect, fairness, and the opportunity to be rewarded for work well done.

CONCLUSION, IMPLICATIONS AND THE TASK AHEAD

Today, our approach to organizational life in uncertain times requires more than one narrow approach. It is necessary to look at a strategic revitalization perspective for integrating ideas regarding quality of work life, technology, structure, leadership, and ways of motivating and rewarding employees. We must find new opportunities for developing all our productive assets. More important, our organizations need effective, proactive programs for employee health promotion and human resource development: We need strategies that foster creative problem solving, strategic thinking, experimentation, good communication, risk taking, realistic planning and empowerment through collaboration. In addition, our organization must develop improved awareness of the forces that operate to limit their true potential: old metaphors, models, frozen attitudes and incompetent systems.

The task is no less than stimulating the organizational imagination, thinking, and critical concern with the complex and interdependent nature of organizational life. We need to devise ways of supporting participation, forms of collaborative work relations, goal-directed feedback, and opportunities for enhancing organizational traditions and values, ways of fostering care, compassion, service, spirit, commitment, excellence and productivity.

The challenge of creating energized, compassionate, productive and quality minded people and organizations is intimately tied with managing the challenges of change. This crucible often brings out the latent potential of organizational members at all levels. We need to explore new and more effective strategies for tapping into these resources in our search for new ways of promoting organizational learning for the uncertain times ahead. This mission will guide the future chapters of this text.

2

THE OPEN SYSTEM

INTRODUCTION

Organizations are composed of systems that are labeled in many ways. The model or framework that we will utilize as a common starting point is call open systems (O.S). Understanding and applying this model will give us both a method and perspectives for designing more effective organizational tasks, programs, and policies.

The framework helps us to answer two important questions. First, what kind of organizational design, structure and shape (including processes) do we need for more productive and effective organizational systems, and how can the design of an effective system assist us in this task? Second, how do we achieve our organizational and system-wide goals for productivity and competitive advantage, without losing sight of the important place that individuals have in the process?

THE OPEN SYSTEM: A WORKING MODEL

Building models of entire organizational systems and its parts or sub-systems is not just an academic exercise. Models allow us to view the complex arrangements of variables under ideal conditions. By creating a working model, we can discover target points that will, hopefully, enable us to understand how we can do practical things that make a difference in our search for competitive success. The building of practical open system models can be improved by utilizing practical research tools, like action research.

Kurt Lewin, one of the founding fathers of organization development (O.D.) and group dynamics, believed that through such a comprehensive change program and action research methods that involvement and commitment to action could be increased, while organizational problems were being solved (Gutknecht and Miller, 1986: 205). Solving problems, thus, becomes an exercise in thinking theoretically about the change process in organizations.   Remember what Lewin said about theory: "There's nothing so practical as good theory."

Like Lewin's action research framework, our open systems model tries to do more than merely explain complex relationships because it must also be simple enough for practitioners to utilize. It must constitute a framework for action, allowing us to visualize how things can work, and suggest methods and technologies to improve deficient outcomes. Following Lewin once again, we know that when we work effectively together, we are more likely to receive support for implementing our programs or policies later in the process.

This is one of most important principles for open systems thinking-- we must do our work with people and the entire system, not to them. Getting the organizational members at all levels on board our organizational or quality improvement train is the key action research and systems design issue.   The issue sounds simple, but the realities are quite different.

Organizational work is highly interdependent and can be done in many ways because it has many components, including inputs, transformation processes technology, outputs, purposes, tasks, values, structure, and the external environment. We can combine these components in many contingent possibilities. There is no one best way to organize.

In a well-designed organization the goals may vary, but productive output is one key essential. People cannot make a productive contribution when absent, ill, excessively stressed by overwork or poorly-designed jobs, lacking a clear vision of the mission, and when supported by autocratic management styles.

SYSTEM DIMENSIONS

Let us now briefly review and expand upon some of the key dimensions and functions performed in each of the organization's component systems. The emphasis is upon the interrelated tasks that all organizational systems must perform in order to maximize their potential for working productively and with dignity. These ideas are meant as only a beginning.

The organization's vision and purpose (we will discuss these shortly) provide continuity and direction for the organization's mission, business plan and goal setting process. The budget is merely the business plan stated in financial targets for accountability. The organization's strategic direction must gain credibility and support through its link with the organizations culture (symbols, values, knowledge, styles of discourse and dress, rituals and myths). The organization also exists in an environment (both internal and external) that influences choices about strategies, tactics and policies.

Many behaviors and processes (communication, conflict management, teamwork, motivation) help management, administrators, and leaders to effectively and efficiently structure activities and processes to accomplish organizational goals. We may label this organizational structure in many ways: divisions and units, number of levels, basis for grouping units, coordinating mechanisms, spatial arrangement of units, activities, human resource policies, power coalitions and union relations.

Inputs (like financial assets, capital assets, cash assets, and human resources) must be transformed through technologies (education, training, health risk assessment, guided imagery, assembly line, batch production, CAD/CAM design, computer assisted instruction) into outputs (products, services, skills, and behaviors) such as increasing profits, improved morale and community image, reduced absenteeism, turnover, and heart disease. Each description depends upon what system level we have chosen to focus upon, from the macro overview to the micro particular.

Each system must select, and train (or rely upon another appropriate system) its personnel to meet goals and match income to expenses to achieve some level of profit or returnof investment. Systems provide the expertise to research, design, develop, market and distribute their products and services both internally and externally.

For example, the health promotion system must use appropriate technology and the work of other systems (training, benefits, medical) to transform knowledge/information resources (inputs determined by needs assessment) into products, services or outputs (like a health awareness fair, a new corporate policy on smoking, or a full blown, comprehensive health promotion program). Most of these products will be used internally by the organization, but some may be marketed externally.

Finally, boundaries are necessary to identify what is within or outside each system. They help define each part of the larger system as a sub-system. Trying to determine the proper boundaries and location for either work or programs is a major leadership responsibility and requires the assistance of line management and human resource staff professionals.

THE HEALTH PROMOTION SYSTEM: A NEW PARTNER FOR PRODUCTIVITY

Let's explore one brief example here and elaborate upon it a little later. The health promotion system (H.P.) provides essential services to the organization in order to insure that employees remain healthy, effective, and productive. The fully developed H.P. system, like the management system, includes all the purposes, structures, policies, procedures, goals, objectives, communication links, human resources, budgets, facilities, and records of accomplishment that any other system includes.

The health promotion system, like other organizational systems, can exist at many levels of development. A small or beginning system might try to use a limited budget, part-time personnel and volunteers to do a preliminary feasibility/needs assessment or try to raise the awareness of other employees through newsletters, posters, flyers, contests, etc. With a bigger budget, and backed by a needs assessment (which could emphasize what goals and impacts are desired), the health promotion system could obviously hire its own consultants and become more sophisticated in the type and range of services, and programs offered (Gutknecht,1988).

H.P. professionals must learn to ask questions like: how can we improve the general organizational system and its goals by using the health promotion system as a force for positive change and innovation? They must also learn how to stimulate a more creative interrelationship of system interaction through health promotion design.

Health promotion professionals can also assist in the process of more productive personal goal attainment and positive behavioral change. The technologies used in health promotion system and programs are varied--the health risk appraisal, cost-containment strategies, a feasibility study or needs assessment, the dissemination of health information, behavioral change strategies, a video orientation session, high-blood pressure screening, dietary programs for modifying negative health (blood pressure and smoking) and even ideas about the influence of the organization upon worker productivity (stress, morale, turnover).

THE ADVANTAGES USING THE OPEN SYSTEM PERSPECTIVE

The open systems model begins when you first see the world through the eyes of another. It is relational and interdisciplinary in the best sense of these words. The approach shows us in the most vivid ways that every world view is, in itself (separated from the whole), terribly restricted. We are all essentially in this world together. There are really no isolated experts or parts (interaction and teamwork are required) in a world of increasing complexity and interdependence. This does not mean that we may not still create our own arrangements of system parts (all good leaders do it anyway), or that we must always agree. The key is learning how to manage such disagreement in order to mobilize our best and diverse talents to master the challenges of change.

The functions that open systems perform reside in our perception of how the organizational parts interact, and what they need to accomplish. Thus, the parts must learn to more effectively listen, sense change, develop peripheral vision, and become more directly involved in the entire organization.

Organizational leaders(chapter8) must certainly learn how to listen, ask questions, accurately perceive, and communicate what is happening in various systems. Involving people is not a game, but the foundation of all good management. It also requires great skill at goal setting, planning, communication, feedback, and social experimentation.

People should be recognized and valued in open systems. They provide needed vision, motivation, meaning and energy to the system. They also make the system more complex because anyone can learn negative norms: hiding information, the consequences of greedy or self-centered actions, even productivity sapping inaction. Feedback in open organizational systems is important; this is perhaps why traditional scientific management approaches and rigid, bureaucratic behavior seems less relevant to workers today.

THE FOUNDATION FOR VISION, VALUES AND MEANING: A PRACTICAL PHILOSOPHY FOR PRODUCTIVITY AND WELLNESS

Effective organizations know how to link vision, values, structures, with effective management behaviors, skills and styles of interaction in a purposeful manner. They know how to build a practical management and human resources philosophy for productive action. The foundation is the establishment of a vision that stands for a preferred future and inspires the discovery of what we really want to accomplish. We then feel motivated to do the necessary work to implement that vision which truly inspires us.

The visionary direction is guided by a philosophy of how effective, productive and humane people and organizations should work together.   This vision is developed into a mission statement (a statement about what business functions we really want to focus upon), then reduced to general aims, and finally, to long-term, mid-term and short-term objectives or measurable goals that are operationally defined through the financial planning process.

The vision can also provide a framework for discovering how serving the organization can also support joint interests and mutual values: a philosophy or partnership for productivity.   Everyone needs to evaluate their fundamental vision about healthy and productive living and working.

The visionary statement about values or important principles should guide our business plan, financial strategies, and all organizational efforts.   Such a general philosophy will add a healthy zest and vitality to our life and our work.   Such a motivational purpose can also promote a new sense of challenge and direction for moving our energies into new domains of the modern information age and to more positive work and lifestyle options.

Good leadership and management always begins with an awareness of why we work. We work for those dreams and opportunities that inspire us to get excited about and care deeply about doing something well. The work world is increasingly chaotic, but solutions exist for dealing with this disorder. Any authentic growth or change begins from within our healthy sense of self-esteem and values. It also requires, as we have already mentioned, our authentic involvement and participation.

If the world appears out of control, it is because we as individuals are out of control, drifting, without the courage to support a healthy vision. We need to become more involved, healthy and productive.
It is up to our leaders today to provide a vision which has aims and purposes to inspire us to high-performing and worthwhile actions. We must learn to link the healthy and effective enterprise with a sense of personal performance and contribution.

Any vision must inspire and provide the vitality, energy and direction for our daily tasks. It also helps us to identify common values and become responsible for our own actions, which diminishes the need for external controls and close supervision. Because this vision must be communicated clearly through all organizational activities, it opens channels for dialogue and feedback, captures our imagination and guides our behavior into positive and optimistic pursuits.

We work brilliantly at that which meets our mutual needs, interests and dreams. In order to encourage this process to take hold, we must evaluate how our leaders promote the linkages between personal performance and organizational productivity. Only well designed channels of dialogue and communication show a leaders comittment to articulate a vision of joint success and well-being. For it is only through open and authentic communication that we are able to link together common efforts that promote organizational goal effectiveness.

Many organizations today are beginning to discuss such issues as management styles which can either encourage or discourage this vision of optimal performance. We are all responsible for creating innovative and flexible systems that allow us to reach our personal potential, remain adaptable and achieve our personal life agenda.

Building better designed and more productive institutional, organizational and community systems should be a worthy goal. Only by designing well and improving system effectiveness, will we allow workers to link their personal effectiveness with the organization's successes and failures.

THE PERSONAL AND ORGANIZATIONAL CONSEQUENCES OF IGNORING PURPOSE

There are many negative consequences that result from blocking this sense of personal health, meaning, autonomy, and personal goal attainment. We find that individuals begin to lose their enthusiasm, energy and ability to work smarter. Organizations lose their power focus on essential tasks with any vigor or effectiveness.

THE CHALLENGE OF CREATING HEALTHY WORK SYSTEMS

How do we organize our organizational systems to stay open, flexible and healthy? Can we learn to facilitate more fruitful options and support systems for building more productive and effective individuals and organizations?

We must begin by discussing how we organize and design our systems for the creative, flexible, and adaptable use of material, people, values, ideas, knowledge, physical space, technology, time and information. We can learn to arrange these resources in more effective and creative ways in order to promote healthy people, improved systems, and stronger, more responsive work cultures.

For example, we can learn how to facilitate better communication and teamwork between individuals, teams and systems. We can explore how management and work practices might contribute to more effective goal attainment, time management and increased personal productivity (the amount of productive work that we can get out of input resources) leading to greater confidence and self-esteem.

If we are to improve the quality of life, health and work for our employees, then we must remember that they need to enjoy an active, healthy, well-balanced and meaningful life beyond the organization. We must invest in our human capital and build upon that which makes each of us care about living productively each day. We must teach people how to balance their work and family life and also model this behavior ourselves.

This idea does not mean we are needlessly encouraging self-indulgent behavior. On the contrary, we can learn to promote those values and skills for participating, enriching, promoting, helping, sharing, adapting, listening, trusting, responding and delegating. These enduring qualities, not temporary, narrow skills, are demanded by the forces of change that impact business and organizational culture today. This organizational view depends upon how we support the wellness and productive potentials of our working people.

The healthy organization will help us to establish a framework and procedures for increasing both personal productivity and organizational effectiveness. It will also assist us to attend to the development of healthy character/values in our children and fellow workers. Our organizations will then be able to utilize human capital to manage change with agility.

Remember, one primary outcome of any effective organization is a more flexible and knowledgeable management culture. This supportive culture enhances both personal and organizational health, development and productivity. These leaders/managers are skilled in the ability to synthesize and create creative, yet productive systems. But we must learn to focus upon both the individual and organization in order to succeed.

DEVELOPING GOALS TARGETS AND PROGRAMS

Good program development, whether we call it personal, human resource or management development, utilizes the power of goals. Goals help us to learn how to prioritize. This helps us to determine where we want to go within a certain time frame and evaluate when we've arrived. Goals are the targets for the energies of individuals, systems, and programs. Goal setting is target practice. It provides an excellent tool regarding our progress toward important life and work priorities.

Goals are not the accomplishments themselves. Goals only help organize the direction o four efforts. Activity may occur without people realizing goals However, without clear direction, feedback and supporting information, we often find activities that merely provide a excuse for failure, not accomplishment or outcomes.

Programs (like training or management development) are the step-by-step process that lead to goal attainment. Programs are a necessary component of every effective system (the training or educational systems). If a program is created to change unproductive unhealthy behavior (smoking or stress), then the goals should measure some accomplishments (quitting smoking, reducing smoking behavior or stress), not just the participation: (ie."yes, I took a smoking reduction or stress class and learned some great things.")

In any service system (marketing, education, consulting) goals are not easily definable, and there is a tendency to confuse programs (behavior, work, therapy, education) with outcomes, like productivity, improved health, weight loss, measurable quality improvement, or cost containment. Programs are the specific means (strategies, plans of action, content areas, like smoking reduction or quality improvement) used to accomplish goals (like, losing 10 lbs., creating a zero- defect rate). They allow us to organize various program or task components in order to achieve goals.

We are not interested in just creating programs. We are interested in building a system that fits with the work culture, helps the organization to achieve its diverse goals (effectiveness). Thus, when we create programs, like a new training or health promotion program, we must show how it will improve goal attainment for both individual workers and the entire system.

Goals often serve as the objects of much conflict and debate. This is because many internal and external groups have a stake in the direction and goals of the organization. We can call such groups, stakeholders (not stockholders who are owners), and we must examine these groups and their values, interests resources and positions for their potential impacts and strategic importance.

Sometimes the involvement of various interest groups, sponsors, participants or other stakeholders makes goal setting seem impossible. Bureaucratic and political infighting surfaces because leaders have failed to set and direct the framework and appropriate mechanisms to allow productive disagreement to improve the final product.

When the various employee factions can not agree on directions or expectations for a program, then prospects of a crisis are likely. At this point strategy is less important than finding the organization's aim, purpose or direction. In order to develop such a direction, leaders and managers must possess good negotiating and communication skills so they can set realistic goals and divert a crisis.

The specific strategy or plan is less important than the guiding vision or direction of the organization. It is not disagreement that is dangerous, but the lack of direction and procedures for provide some grounds for resolving disagreements. Direction provided by supportive and innovative leaders, will generally allow differences to be worked out in the concrete process of deciding the most productive goals and program pathways to pursue.

MANAGEMENT FOR PRODUCTIVE RESULTS

Effective management development programs can be designed for various levels of employee involvement. Top leaders should be involved in some manner and set the tone by communicating the vision. A clear and positive vision establishes the context for demonstrating the potential benefits for each level of employee and in their own language.

Effective management development, training and educational programs require that the aims, components and procedures be clearly understood by all involved. This is what we mean by building a supportive culture or environment. Decision making should be shared, if possible, with participants, who help decide the topics, programs, kinds of promotional efforts and general scheduling.

If all managers understand the important aims and benefits of the programs, there is a greater chance that they will develop more challenging personal goals. Even if you cannot convince managers that attending the program is an optimal use of their time, at least you have allowed them the opportunity to express what they feel is important to include in the course. This strategy may help you to enlist their recommendation and possible future support.

The management development program must assist the individual to pursue effective personal development and career goals. Somehow, organizations need to return to the idea that people's work is not their entire life, but only something that they choose to productively pursue. The growth of the whole manager then becomes one of our main concerns.

We do not yet know why an organization would so easily destroy the seeds of such an important idea, but we can speculate that it is probably the same reason that productivity suffers in many organizations today: control, lack of goals or objectives; poor and inadequate feedback; failure to match personal values and strengths to the task; excessive fear of failure; lack of cultural support for innovative behavior and practices; and failure to provide the right information for effective performance. All of these problems begin with a failure of vision in overly rigid, bureaucratic settings.

THE MANAGER OF THE FUTURE

Leaders must learn to set the design climate and managers must learn to think through the practical process that facilitates more adaptable, creative, meaningful and productive work environments. To get results or productive improvements, we need to support all those programs that assist workers to increase their energy and vitality, and that support balanced, resourceful, enriched and healthy lives.

Managers and leaders can begin by managing their own health, wellness and energy with a vision that builds upon their own wellness potential. Getting people in the right programs and jobs so their talents and strengths are used is another dimension of the task ahead. Then workers will perceive their own opportunities for wellness and productivity everywhere, experience measurable success and motivate themselves.

Those desiring to develop and administer management development programs must start to rethink the appropriate values, skills, information, roles and responsibilities for bringing out the productive potential of our changing work force. The role requirements are varied, but the general description is: competent to design flexible and innovative systems and programs. The role description will matter less than the ability of the person to effectively bring together appropriate resources to get the work done productively.

This person will be a practical and resourceful, a generalist and a specialist, and capable of using existing systems, processes and procedures to full advantage. He or she will have deep enough professional knowledge to function like a conductor; orchestrating and arranging important processes, tools, structures, skills, and managerial expertise. He or she will strategically take advantage of various organizational options.

This leader/manager will function more as a project director and less as a controller. We are talking about the need for an organizational designer who can provide the cohesion and direction for operations, temporary teams, planning groups, committees, marketing, promotion and program execution. Thus, managing with people rather than for or to them will become one of the more important requisites of this challenging role.

This art of synthesis will demand people who know how to integrate and link disparate system elements, without allowing them to either lose their unique aspects or disintegrate into purposeless and soulless organizational deadwood. As a generalist, the modern professional manager will understand how to utilize other specialists to spread their abilities over larger systems, space, time and distance without diluting their talents. As a specialist, the manager will know the general professional parameters that provide very useful and practical real world examples to guide other professionals. It never hurts for leaders to wow them with a little in-depth professional expertise (expert power) now and again.

The key question for leadership/management development programs of the future are: What visions, directions, supports, training, programs, information, performance assistance, health goal feedback, and sponsorship can we provide our workers? And how can we learn to build upon their strengths as we assist them to achieve health, vitality, comittment, and productivity?

Successful programs will spawn healthy organizations and optimally healthy and successful people will reverse the direction of influence. After all, this is an open system view. But for now, let's return to some topics that more closely relate to improving individual performance.

3

A FRAMEWORK FOR ACTIVE LEARNING:

INTRODUCTION

Active learning requires our active participation in expanding our knowledge. In our professional and organizational environments, we have a significant responsibility for expanding our professional boundaries. Active learning skills help us to assess our needs and abilities, set professional and personal goals, integrate information, implement plans for change, obtain feedback, identify resources, and evaluate what we have learned.

Active learning is a process of utilizing information, ideas, and knowledge to meaningfully adapt, respond and innovate. Active learning requires that we seek out diverse sources of information, perceptions, goals, plans, strategies, and skills, and take time to consolidate, construct and integrate knowledge that insures a foundation for future learning.

Establishing contacts, synthesizing and bridging to new ideas and technologies can help us to solidify our commitment to effectively managing information for human resource development all at levels of organization and society. In utilizing the fruits of such an information and knowledge revolution, we need to remain humble at the door of learning; open to new technologies, yet aware of their abuses and limits.

By opening ourselves to new technologies and perspectives on learning and information, we prepare ourselves for the responsibility of becoming more adaptable when faced with continuous change. It also helps us to deal with complexity and uncertainty because we will be able to see the world from fresh and responsive viewpoints.

Active learning helps us to recognize the systematic interrelationships of interlocking problems. Oftcn as we try to solve problems, we find that they become larger and more complex. To deal with these nested layers of complexity, we must know how to use all the stages of active learning.

The more we understand and use the active learning process, the better equipped we are to master a new domains of knowledge. The active learning stages are *assessment, goal setting, integration, implementation, feedback, resource identification and evaluation.* These processes provide a framework for understanding activities, such as designing human resource, training or health promotion programs. This seven stage process of active learning may occur in a continuous cycle, shift at uneven intervals, repeat themselves or occur out of order, depending upon our learning goals.

Active learning is a constant, life-long process. In productive organizations, continuous learning is an unwritten policy where everyone is in a permanent state of acquiring relevant information for meeting diverse learning goals. The organization collaborates with each employee through the exchange of relevant information, ideas, knowledge and experience. This exchange allows important new ideas to become effectively implemented within the organization.

However, as the organization faces maturity or restructuring, the knowledge and experience of long-term members must be tapped to assist the organization in developing the courage to absorb the necessary information to face the challenges of change ahead. These seasoned veterans can assist the organization to view change in a positive way.

To successfully implement needed innovation, only the most respected sources can be called upon to act as buffers for the negative impacts of change, and to promote the positive strategic knowledge for the next generation of leaders. This responsibility for the generational transfer of new knowledge is a task only reserved for the most respected and competent leaders available, whether formal or informal, because it prepares the organization to effectively face continuous change.

Continuous active learning assumes that learning is also an important part of everyone's job and is practiced each day. It involves a sort of job enrichment policy, in that employees must rely on the knowledge and expertise of their leaders and co-workers to understand how they can improve their own job performance. An understanding of the relationship between their work and the way the whole organization does business is crucial for employees who wish to master some of the impacts of change on their own jobs.

Understanding these organizational realities is the goal of active learning; making it work will produce personal and organizational results. This sort of organizational renewal multiplies through a process of highly responsive interaction. In addition, all workers not only become more responsible for learning from their co-workers, but they also become more responsible for teaching their co-workers what they know.

ACTIVE LEARNING THROUGH PARTICIPATION

Active participation improves our desire to broaden our perspective about managing the growth and development of employees. People who participate actively are more autonomous and more self-directed than those who rely on a superlative source to point them to and walk them down the paths they must follow to success.

For example, take a worker who wants to prepare himself for a new assignment or promotion. He knows that competent workers can earn promotions, but is not sure the steps to take to find more challenging assignments in order to prove himself. He decides to ask for guidance and adapts his strategies to the realities around him. In the final analysis, he finds that despite knowing about the bosses opinions and general organizational policies, the final decision was made by him/herself. .

Now, as simple as it may seem to us, this operation could have failed in several ways. Since the truly active participant is accountable for his own decisions, if the worker had failed in his chosen activities, as a true active participant he would be required to take full responsibility for not making use of his resources (his boss, co-workers, knowledge of organizational politics or policies), although he might try to blame others for his failure.

The active participant learns to welcome with excitement the challenge of trying something new. With a greater degree of direction, he is able to learn more while still acting reponsibly.

Active participation throughout the organization helps to ensure successful learning and and higher achievement. Active participation requires that we create more opportunities for learning the skills relevant for active learning: including enlarged job responsibilities, new forms of communication, and how to productively use new forms of technological and information innovation. Active learning about our jobs, organizations and industries is increased through the process of participation and delegation. Here are some **action strategies** for improving your delegating skills.

DELEGATING STRATEGIES

* For any task you are considering delegating to someone, first evaluate theemployee's developmental level and probable stage of readiness.
* Be sure you fully understand the task to be delegated.
* Divide the task into segments that generally involve the follow ing stages:
    1) Could perform a single carefully delineated task;
    2) Could anticipate the manager's future needs, in addition to above;
    3) Is able to participate meaningfully in planning, problem solving and evaluation of task;
    4) Is able to handle successfully the complex task from

planning to evaluation without supervision and feedback;
* Explain clearly what you want done, how you want it done, why you want it done, when you want it done and with whom the employee should interact;
* Gain the employee's commitment to the task by encouraging participation;
* Show trust and support throught the process;
* Set up progress checkpoints;
* Jointly review the work. Reinforce correctly implemented tasks or parts of tasks.

ASSESSMENT

The key to assessment is awareness. We must have self awareness, awareness of others around us and of our environment to begin to succeed as an active learner. When we have self-awareness we are able to improve the self-assessment of our strengths and weaknesses and priorities. This helps us to determine our greatest needs for learning. It gives us a clearer understanding of how we function in our environment and how we might improve our performance. By appraising or assessing our strengths, weaknesses and needs, we are able to gain a sense of purpose and direction for our learning. We can then move ahead more rapidly as we act upon these discovered learning priorities.

Assessing our needs reduces wasted effort; we now learn of what we need know. This enables us to quickly determine questions that lead us to the knowledge and skills we must acquire. Actively assessing our needs involves conducting a systematic review of both our present skill levels and goal priorities for learning acquisition. The more specifically we define our needs, interests, skill and knowledge requirements, the easier it is to develop methods for fulfilling them (i.e., goal setting).

Self-assessment becomes an excellent measurement tool for determining personal and professional growth and development. It requires that we personally identify specific skills and knowledge requirements. Next, we must devise a rationale for selecting each skill requirement and illustrate to ourselves (via lists of examples) how we might use or integrate for future innovation this skill or knowledge.

By formulating a rating system for determining the importance of each knowledge unit, research project, training or skill program, we can determine our strengths, weaknesses and needs. By determining our needs we can now clutter the stage with another active learning prop: goal setting.

GOAL SETTING AND TAGETING

Goal setting can simply be described as plotting a course of action and shooting at a target. It requires a great deal of forethought and planning. Reaching a goal can be done in several ways. Also there are several reasons why certain goals fail to be reached. To begin to achieve a goal it is necessary to understand skills, needs, consequences, obstacles and resources which affect the attainment of the desired target.

Active learners participate in their learning by setting goals to give them a sense of direction, a script of sorts. They set their goals because they know that they are responsible for parts in life they would like to play successfully--being a good parent, husband, worker, writer, college president, tennis player, teacher, etc. They also need to know what targets and roles will help them grow in their chosen direction. The targets or goals people choose to follow should be based on the results of their self-assessment analysis, as described in the preceding section.

When we attain the targets we set, we get a sense of completion, inspiration and feedback for repositioning our energies. When we don't attain a goal, however, it is not a complete loss. Unattained targets can be useful feedback and provide us with further information concerning our unmet needs. Targets can also act as reference points to show what adjustments in actions or behavior we must make in order to get closer to the bullseye.

In target setting it is important to choose realistic ones. We should choose targets which are in concurrence with our abilities to complete whatever actions are necessary to achieve those targets. Choosing simple targets indicates a lack of self-confidence and even, perhaps, unproductive work habits. In contrast, the selection of difficult targets may, at least near the end of the work effort, cause a drop in motivation. Realistic targets, however, provide us with motivational stress, a sort of "sweet tension," that is required for making a successful bull's eye.

Usually when we aim poorly at a target there is a good reason for doing so. The target may indeed be a badly chosen one. It is also possible that the target is not clearly perceived as a legitimate one. When managers set goals with their workers, it is important that everyone agrees on the importance of the goal.

Sometimes an aim can be perfect, but the effort falls short and the goal is not reached. Somewhere along the way there is not enough energy to keep the effort propelled so it can reach its target. A shortfall like this can be due to personal and internal factors such as poor motivation or unrealistic targets or from system problems like-- group and organizational conflicts, communication breakdowns or departmental boundary disputes, resistance by the customer to a new product or service, and the realities of a competitive market-place.

It is important to determine honestly whether the failure to reach the target is due to internal or external factors, especially when there may be a mixture of both. Often when there is a mixture, we tend to blame the whole problem on the external factors. Often, choosing an intermediate target can prove itself to be a genuine target. It is genuine in that it enhances motivation to continue and strive toward reaching the end target. For awhile, an intermediate target can become a complete aim in itself.

To reach a goal on target, it is important that we establish a strategy to keep us aiming correctly. The best strategy to guard against failure is establishing broad guidelines. They should be just broad enough, however, to allow reasonable flexibility in direction. Guidelines that are too broad aren't real guidelines When guidelines are too broad, they can cause an overshooting of the target. When guidelines are too narrow or rigid, they defeat their purpose. They aren't guidelines either, but rather a straight shot to the target, without any flexibility for intermediate decision making or the achievement of intermediate targets. Guidelines (Gutknecht and Miller, 1986:130- 131) should only be as broad as their targets. Here are some **action learning hints** for better goal setting (or goal practice).

SETTING USABLE GOALS
* Emphasizes results, not activities
* Is measurable
* Is challenging but achievable
* Is in writing
* Is linked to other organizational goals, mission and vision
* Is mutually agreed upon
* Is periodically reviewed and revised, if necessary

ELEMENTS OF A WELL-WRITTEN GOAL
* Who will achieve goal?
* What action will be taken?
* What the measurable key result will be?
* What the target date is set for completion?

BASIC STRATEGIES FOR TALKING ABOUT GOALS
Stage One: Getting ready to set goals
Stage Two: The joint goal setting meeting/discussion
Stage Three: Periodic goal progress review
Stage Four: Final goal attainment review and appraisal

Setting goals is also an excellent way to reduce stress and increase motivation. However, failure to develop flexible procedures can lock workers into choosing dysfunctional goals, particularly in changing environments. The resulting pressure and stress can reduce the attainment of important organizational goals as well. On the other hand, goal setting is an excellent means to reduce frustration and procrastination. It is alright to change goals. For instance, if you are bored with the long-range goals you once set (you might desire a career change, or you might desire to break old ties), then decide to get out of your old ruts by accepting that new and challenging opportunity.

Goal setting allows us the opportunity to explore the world, to gamble and risk failure for the gratification of tangible feedback, and unlimited growth opportunities. In fact, how we perceive risk and failure reveals startling clues about our motivation, personality, lifestyles and coping patterns. Individuals need to learn how to view their failures as learning experiences. By using follow up evaluations and feedback, they can then put failure in perspective and sharpen their future chances for success

This positive feedback provides an opportunity to reformulate goals, evaluate errors, and continue to learn. Guilt over our inadequacies just gets in the way. We don't fail as individuals; we only fail to achieve specific goals. In fact, by reaching for difficult goals, we learn more about ourselves and the world than we knew before.

Goal setting is an opportunity for each of us to get in touch with our skills, values, needs, purposes, wants, dreams and current level of knowledge and information. In addition, the process requires us to explore the world more vigoriously. Before anyone sets out to design their world, in the short-or long-run, they need to know how they currently view their own work lives, purposes and dreams. Goal setting also facilitates better decision making because at least we are more aware of our personal weaknesses and strengths and how they sometimes cause us to foreclose upon excellent opportunities for expanding our learning environment.

Let's explore a few simple **action strategies** that might give us some clues about our work style capabilities and purposes. Ask yourself: are you strong enough to make improvements based upon this assessment; after receiving feedback from others can you achieve your priority goals without giving away personal power? Do you perceive your strong features as well as your weak ones? What kind of work and life goals would you risk to set over a short-term (1day to 6 months), medium-term (6 months to 2 years), and long-term (2-10 years)?

In addition, it is important to examine your psychological and spiritual interior world. Setting goals can help us stop wasted activity, going through the motions, in order to introspect a bit more. After all, we must learn how to sometimes just say *not now* to our outward directed, highly mobile, and achievement orientated culture. We need to take time to reflect upon our unique innner qualities, strengths, potentials, skills, values and beliefs. Let's examine one tool that might help us to accomplish this task..

One tool is a **self-image map (collage)** about yourself. Select your images without analyzing or thinking . You can find pictures, graphics, symbols, words, phrases that reflect your values, interests, hobbies, fantasies, career directions, view of success, needs, wants, desires, fears, and values. Make sure when you assemble self-image map in a creative manner, following Buzan's (1974:90) idea of brain patterns and creative effort:

> *In creative efforts of this nature the mind should be left as "free" as possible. Any thinking about where things should go or whether they should be included will simply slow down the process. The idea is to recall everything your mind thinks of.*

A second tool is a **goal setting time line**. List your five highest priorities or major personal, spritual and professional concerns. Each priority must have a motivation important enough to build a goal around. Next, list activities which are important to you under these areas and focus upon: family, career, financial, health, and educational dimensions.

Understanding your work, career and life priorities is the first step in setting meaningful goals. Many individuals ignore the importance of formulating goals in favor of focusing on the process of constantly changing them. Ask yourself if these goals are really important and worth investing energy in their pursuit.

Make up your plan for goal attainment, be specific regarding the ways of reaching your goals. Make sure your tactics fit your work-life tasks and priorities, but allow yourself to reach outside of comfortable behaviors to set greater goals. Break down goals into sub-components, so that short-term goals feed into your medium and long-term goals.

The Toastmasters International formula for successful speaking is a good blueprint for successful goal attainment. First, follow the rule: Listen, talk, act. Collect relevant information, organize it and act. Second, develop enthusiasm about your goal. Third, visualize having attained your goal. Fourth, work towards your goals in the present, as if you have already achieved them. Living your goal attainment before it actually happens can build self-esteem and start a positive, self-fulfilling prophecy regarding your ability to attain your goals. Our expectations about success or failure certainly influence our chances for attaining or failing to attain our goals.

INTEGRATION

Integration is the combining, selecting and processing of information and experiences. Processing information includes deciding what is to be stored and what is not. Integrating new information and experiences requires time, skill development and the ability to examine one's actions and insights concerning the new information and experiences.

Understanding how to integrate the meaning and usefulness of new information helps to strengthen active learning skills and leads to more effective organizational participation. Integrating new information can be a slow, time consuming process. Often it is difficult to sort through the enormous quantity of information that we receive, so we refrain from additional searching. By developing a framework for organizing the elements of the new information, it is easier to think through their relevance and determine how they relate to other information and experiences.

Tools for developing this framework are notebooks, journals, portable tape recorders, software programs, on-line databases, spreadsheets, integrated word processors (like Full Write Professional), and CD ROM technology. In school we take notes on new data. During meetings we write down important events, concepts and requirements. The recording process could start with a full description of the concept or experience. Next, record or enter key insights, experiences, or new data; this helps to understand how this data relates to our current information needs. Knowing this, we should be able to list the potential uses of any new knowledge, particularly its uses in an organizational setting. Finally, by raising questions concerning the cross referencing of new concepts or experiences, we are using these tools to build new models or frameworks for identifying further information needs.

Setting out to acquire more information requires a high level of motivation and an established learning foundation. The acquisition of new information usually stems from pre-existing knowledge Acquiring general information is a much more difficult process than acquiring specific data. Acquiring general information usually takes a lot of time and experience in a given field. To finally achieve this more liberal approach to learning, specific information is gradually accumulated and integrated using a wide variety of tools and higher level technologies along the way. By noting the specific data and integrating it through more sophisticated processes, we not only improve motivation but open ourselves to higher, more integrated knowledge.

Much information exploring involves linking materials, experiences, ideas, and data together. We strive to find an overall picture which makes the information or experiences more meaningful. Linking information requires active participation in the integration process as we respond to new connections of concepts and events. We must extract information from information and life experience to create knowlege.

More important,, the outcome we each receive from extraction is a unique event, yet one that is easily shared if we desire public confirmation. It is not likely that two people will ever have exactly the same reaction to events or integrate specific information in the same way; but the essence of science relies upon this human dilemma. For this reason, finding support or shared confirmation is an important aspect of actively integrating ideas into structures of knowledge: the primary functions of the scientific method.

Asking questions extends the information field in the direction of the question or hypothesis. Questions help us focus our attention on what we already know and what we do not know. They also help us find the confirmation, additional resources or, information that we need in order to expand the learning process. By seeking answers to our questions, we also seek support or disconfirmation for our ideas.

The scientific method teaches us that when we have an idea, we can check its validity by convincing our peers of its value. This also involves finding various forms of funding and a means of dissemination or publication. Empirical evidence is a good foundation for showing others how we have both valued and validated our ideas; hence, we have grounds for asking others to support them. Integrating information, therefore, involves theoretical, methodological and practical integration, elaboration and dissemination.

We are not used to challenging our comfortable assumptions. Yet, these challenges are what give us breakthroughs in designing new thinking technologies. By developing a habit of critically evaluating our own ideas, we suspend our commitment to the comfortable world of our own making, and become energized by the creative excitement of pursuing some promising new concept. We may even find a degree of respect for that old intellectual or ideological adversary we once thought our nemesis.

Advanced integration requires a new perspective on the information or experience we have integrated. This requires an openness to evidence and the challenging of our pet ideas. It is a difficult activity, perhaps even the most difficult part of the active learning process.

In Japanese business, for instance, the Ringi is a type of group decision making ceremony that involves a process of combining information. Each key organizational member contributes some information until an integrated picture forms that can be consensually validated as an appropriate plan of action. In the western world, business parties offer ideas and solicit support or refutation. This information is used as evidence for decision making. However, in both societies it is often the business culture, rather than the participant, which decides whether information will be used as an item for contradiction, and conflict or as an element for positive teamwork and integration. We knew this lesson in the business world before the Japanese, but it has only recently been revived as a potent adjunct to our entrepreneurial talents.

Once we have constructed a complete chain link or integrated web of information concerning a given subject, we must not develop the impression that we are finished. After any body of knowledge has been developed, we must remember to frequently do several things:

1. Find time to record, write, reflect about information, knowledge, values, interests, ideas, opinions, etc.
2. Review bodies of ideas and knowledge before we lose track of them.
3. Survey the fields of information and experiences which relate to various bodies of knowledge to update them according to recent research and techniques fo integration.
4. Cross reference information through new technologies, like computer data bases, interactive media, CD ROM storage using Hyper Card and Hyper Text developments.

By doing a survey from time to time on things we know, we may find that we can answer questions that we were previously unable to answer. Having acquired more bodies of knowledge and new technologies of integration, we can begin the learning processes all over again at a higher level. Further integration of knowledge will also lead us to design new strategies and techniques for implementing what we have learned. Social enterpreneurs are as important as economic ones (Drucker, 1986), although using them both is now a necessity in a world requiring innovation for survival.

IMPLEMENTATION

Implementation involves putting thoughts and ideas into an active plan. Assessment, goal setting and integration help us to implement a plan for using new technologies, marketing or promoting programs, evaluating their success, modifying unacceptable situations or resolving problems. Implementing such plans takes into account the needs of others who are affected by the plan.

Information alone is not enough to solve problems. It does not think, nor does it generate ideas. Ideas are complex arrays of information which we can put together in varied yet unique ways. We must sort through the information that we gather on the way to consolidating and maximizing its effectiveness. This will help us find the valid and vital information, which will then aid us in our goal attainment; it will also eliminate information which is not particularly useful.

Any arrangement of information can be combined in new ways to generate more creative alternatives for implementing change technologies (see chapter4). Try to *leverage your information* by organizing it in new, customized ways; provide the information when other sources are not available, like at night or on weekends; repackage discarded or misunderstood information. By using information in these ways, we can create alternative approaches to both our information needs and problem solving strategies (Weitzen, 1988).

We are used to thinking in terms of narrow information and problem definitions. By opening up our approach to new sources and organization of information, we prepare ourselves for generating multiple alternatives and solutions to the demands of a changing world. Innovation and productivity is enhanced by arranging information in several ways so we can generate alternative definitions of problems and resulting solutions.

Sometimes multiple problems are mistaken for the same problem because their definitions fall under the same subject heading. Multiple problems under the same heading can easily lead to confusion. So, it is important to think through the problems and concretely distinguish them from one another.   When we find ourselves in this situation, to avoid confusion, it is best to extract each problem and treat it separately, at separate times, even by separate people.   Especially when problems are closely related, we need to approach them with a fresh start and an open mind.

We learned that by making a target broad we are sure to reach it.   A similar situation is true for problem solving.   By approximating a solution we can get a rough idea of it.   Often that is enough because we are limited by cost and time factors.   We do not have all that is necessary to form a precise conclusion.   We satifice or search for the most satisfactory alternative rather than optimize, which is a search for the best one   Later, however, we may need to redefine our problem, and the rough solution we have devised is enough to give us more headway as we proceed to a bigger problem.

FEEDBACK

Feedback, as a means of getting useable, practical information is a productivity tool (Gutknecht and Miller, 1986:134-135).   Tools, like computers) and techniques (like active listening) that improve the feedback and information-seeking process, also improve productivity.   Feedback is a tool for understanding ourselves (self-assessment) and expanding our learning capabilities.   It helps us most when the source is an integral part of our learning environment and planning. When we can provide our own feedback, we also have learned how to actively participate in tapping own learning resources and truly learning for ourselves. By learning this lesson about feedback, we also can design better learning networks.

The most used feedback is internal. Living organisms continually use feedback as one of the most important aspects of their survival system.   However, organizing helps us to move beyond the daily, habitual patterns of living for the immediate present, in order to prepare for the challenges of living for a well-prepared, thoughtful future. We must like with other systems to survive.   If we have a clear picture of the visions which we are organizing or living for and the standards by which we can evaluate them, we can learn how to manage change more productively through appropriate feedback mechanisms (Gutknecht amd Miller, 1986:130-131).

The usefulness of feedback is contingent upon our receptiveness to its information content and our awareness and objectivity concerning what is presented. Ideally, our learning and working situations should give us all the feedback we require, if we use multiple channels for input and encourage the corporate culture to do the same. If we can get feedback this way, we will become less dependent on unreliable sources and channels for information and learning.

There are two specific kinds of interpersonal feedback: confirmatory feedback and corrective feedback. Confirmatory feedback indicates that goals are acceptable in measurable terms such as quantity, quality, timeliness and cost. It also deals with acceptable progress toward a goal or subgoal. For example, a certain clothing distributor may reach the intermediate target of selling more of an item to a certain chain discount store, along the way to increasing the overall market sales in a particular geographical area. Confirmatory feedback confirms and is used to assure us that we are progressing.

Corrective feedback helps us to reach a goal by indicating that a goal has not yet been reached and our progression is not acceptable in the measurable terms stated earlier. For instance, our company president may explain to us that our overall design for a new service system is good, but it lacks some important details necessary for succeeding with distinction. Second, our supervisor would explain to us what he means by "important details" and will assist us in corrective action.

To be most effective, feedback should be as immediate and as specific as possible. When someone else gives us feedback, or we give it to someone else, the giving person must take responsibility for what he is saying. This means that feedback should be an honest response to the learning situation and cultural environment which sustains it.

Feedback should also be given with a basic respect for the other person's well-being and learning integrity. Feedback should be given when the person is most likely to be open to receiving it and should be kept confidential. Confidentiality builds trust. When someone gives us feedback, our trust in that person is a very important component of our being open and receptive to what he or she is telling us.

It is important that corrective feedback be given and approached in a positive way to build the confidence of the recipient. It is important to point out the good aspects of a job as well as the bad; otherwise, the recipient may tend to avoid the corrective feedback process altogether. Here are some practical **active learning strategies** when doing coaching and performance appraisals.

BASIC COACHING MEETING STRATEGIES

* Explain the purpose of the session;
* Ask the employee to describe his/her perspective on the problem;
* Manager describes his/her perspective;
* Ask the employee to compare the perspectives;
* Manager explains what she/he wants from the employee;
* Manager asks what the employee wants from the manager;

STRATEGIES FOR COACHING MEETING FOLLOW-UP

* Ask the employee to review her/his progress;
* State your perceptions;
* Resolve the discrepancies;
* Positivly reinforce any behavior change that has occurred in the desired direction;

BASIC PERFORMANCE APPRAISAL (PA) DISCUSSION STRATEGIES

* Be sociable;
* Discuss the benefits of a problem solving PA to the employee;

* Ask for the employee's self-appraisal;
* Present your own appraisal;
* Confirm the employee's understanding and get reactions;
* Summarize and resolve your agreements and disagreements;
* Discuss goals and action plans for the next performance period;
* Discuss obstacles standing in the way of reaching these goals;
* Recheck understanding and commitment;
* They jointly decide what has to be changed and how to do it;
* A date is set for review.

RESOURCE IDENTIFICATION

Resource identification involves identifying existing and potential resources which can offer supports for reinforcing what we have learned. This requires that we devise a plan for using our resources efficiently. Resources include such items as self-awareness, positive political skills, information, informal contacts, materials, and technology. To be effective learners we must know how to use our resources.

The people who work in the system in which we work are our most important and valuable resources. They use their working knowledge, skills and material resources to implement their goals as they link them with the organization's goals. For instance, teachers use their own knowledge and skills to help others learn how to acquire the methods for life-long learning. Counselors guide us by introducing us to new methods and skills for dealing with and solving our problems. Mentors guide others to follow the appropriate career paths leading to organizational success.

Yet, it is easy to take people's work for granted when considering their resource potential. How often do we consider how much time the people who are our resources must spend to effectively increase their knowledge so they can be helpful to us?

Teachers must have teaching skills to begin with, but must also keep themselves current in their information areas by attending courses, seminars, conferences and other events which help them to develop their profession. Our managers must develop their people-skills and communication skills, increase their knowledge of information strategies and planning, and keep up-to-date in their specific technical areas to continue to be helpful to us and the organization.

When looking to people for support, we must also look beyond the person's degree of "working knowledge," (i.e., his background and expertise). Then we will be able to develop a more exact idea of how this person can give us support. A person's competence, reputable skills and our own compatability with that person are other very important aspects to consider in choosing a mentor.

EVALUATION

Finally, evaluation is the ability to step back from what we have learned and the information we are given and make a judgement as to its meaning, quality, relevance and impact. The evaluation may be a simple as a mental checklist, or as complex as a quantitative analysis.

Certain variables determinee the overall value of a learning experience. Each variable is significant alone and in its interaction with other variables. The variables are grouped into three major categories: content, process and experience. Content variables involve the nature and quantity of information that is presented during the learning experience.

Process variables refer to the process by which the information is presented to us. These include the style and structure of the material, for example, the method of teaching. Process variables can have a significant impact on learning as they may affect our attitudes toward a complete learning experience.

Experience variables refer to events and structures that take into account the participant's actions and reactions. They impact our skill acquisition and even our motivation to understand principles and concepts. Learning experience variables may even impact our interest in transferring it to another life setting, for instance, transferring a skill we learned in our work setting (such as a specific organizational method) to our home life. We will explore this topic in much greater detail in chapter 7 as it pertains to evaluating organizational programs. Patton (1987) provides an excellent analysis on creative evaluation using the following types of strategies:

1. Metaphors;
2. Going with the flow;
3. Matrix and Quandrant thinking;
4. Simulation games and Experiential exercises;
5. Picturethinking;
6. Storytelling;
7. Other creative methods: Participative interview chain, teaching instead of doing;
8. Humor.

CONCLUSION

Active learning help us to analyze our needs and abilities, set professional and personal learning goals, integrate information, implement plans for change, obtain feedback, identify resources, and evaluate what we have learned. This process parallels the organizational learning process which accompanies the development and implementation of organizational training, human resources or health promotion programs. Active learning helps us to recognize the systematic interrelationships of interlocking problems. It requires that we seek out diverse sources of information, perceptions, goals, plans, strategies and skills, and take time to consolidate, construct and integrate knowledge that insures a foundation for future learning.

4

STIMULATING CREATIVE THINKING FOR INNOVATION

INTRODUCTION

Personal and organizational creativity are not deep mysteries penetrated only by a chosen few select geniuses. You can become a more creative leader and manager. Creativity simply refers to the ways of generating new, more unique, or novel ideas and solutions to problems. The failure to find more creativity in organizational life is the result of blockages, and communication gaps, not the lack of high IQ workers.

If we really accept some ridiculous view that creativity is only for some spoiled genius or those with protruding brains, then the message is clear--don't risk effort because you will surely fail, and maybe even humiliate yourself in the process. If this premise is even tacitly supported, innovative and entrepreneurial thinking will surely dry up in most organizations.

The actual facts about creativity are really quite different and should give us much hope. Creativity is not solely related to special personal traits or characteristics, according to experts in the field.

THE DIMENSIONS OF CREATIVITY

Creativity includes such components as imaginatively generating original or novel ideas, utilizing knowledge (gather as much relevant information and other resources as possible) to evaluate the ideas, and finally, working to insure their implementation. Here we find many of the same concepts that were identified in chapter 3, but with a slightly different arrangement. People may be creative in any of the key dimensions, but the success of any creative project or product demands that we recognize all dimensions. For example, we must first develop potentially original ideas. We cannot, however, generate good ideas while saturated with the fear of breaking the organizations cultural beliefs that promoting safe and noncontroversial ideas is the only way to get ahead.

Determining originality is not a game that we should leave to creative types alone. Systematic evaluation of potentially unique ideas usually requires that left-brained, linear thinking types assist us to assist us with the evaluation. This helps us to insure their high quality application to the particular practical problem or situation we are currently exploring. Structuring the proper mix of different thinking types into work teams will enhance the general creativity and effectiveness of individuals and organizations.

Highly original or quality ideas once evaluated and selected, must then be implemented, if they are to make a difference. This task requires good planning, communication and change management skills. Many individuals forget that reducing the resistance to creative ideas and fostering their implementation through innovative srvices or products is as important as generating good ideas in the first place.

Workers in uncreative, unproductive, and highly bureaucratic organizations often learn that doing nothing, obstructing innovation, or avoiding risks are the consistently rewarded behaviors. Remember, any positive change must be reinforced through the reward system (compensation, performance appraisal, bonuses, recognition) and modeled by respected leaders and managers. When this doesn't happen, it is customary for workers in such situations to avoid any suspect behavior, including creative or entrepreneurial actions. Soon people stop taking risks or developing creative ideas.

Creativity, intrapreneurship (enterpreneurs working in large organizations, rather than starting their own businesses) and innovation must go together, if we desire our ideas to be implemented. Innovations are the changes made in opposition to the established, habitual, and routine ways of operating. Innovation combines the various dimensions of the creative process into marketable products or services, so that real improvements become implemented and achieve concrete results.

A primary task of anyone trying to use creativity to harness innovation is to sort out those situations which are crucial. It is easier to build relevance into a creative ideas than vice-versa, because the first key process is breaking through the barriers that have prevented a workable new direction from emerging out of the daily refrain to follow standard operating procedures.

WHAT IS CREATIVITY: A VIEW FROM OUR PAST

Creative thinking is like looking through a kaleidoscope when we were kids. As we turned the barrel of the kaleidoscope the loose, jagged colored glass changed into fantastic, unique shapes and patterns that caused the joyous morning hours to flow effortlessly into the warming afternoon without much notice. Why can't adults feel the same way about the way they work and live?

This image helps us to visualize a picture of the receptive worker or organization: open to ideas, supported in the attempt to form old ideas into new patterns and arrangements. As the creative person twists reality, changes perspective, and maybe even develops a new angle on an old problem, a vague, intuitive feeling catches this person by surprise.

We are all only limited by our self-confidence and ability to imagine and rearrange reality. That is what creativity is all about! By twisting the kaleidoscope or shifting the way we define problems and see the world, we gain more control over our work and personal effectiveness.

Good management, like human resource development, training or even health promotion, is really concerned with opportunities for practicing creativity on the firing line. Creativity can support some very practical goals which will help us to improve our personal well-being and organizational productivity. But we need to know how to use our creative skills to manage and develop people and systems by removing the blocks to creative thinking and innovative action.

BLOCKS TO PLAY WITH AND PUT AWAY

Why aren't leaders, managers and workers more creative? The answer is not because they are incapable. Instead, we need to look at those learned habits that have become blocks to our natural creativity and openness to different ways of viewing the world around us. By understanding some of these blocks, we can better prepare to learn some creative techniques for improving the personal well-being of workers, as well as increasing organizational effectiveness.

Ask yourself, "how do I perceive the situation?" **Perceptual blocks** are like invisible walls that keep us from seeing all the possibilities in the situation. For example, do you check your style of communication when others fail to seem to listen and follow your instructions?

The perceptual block lies in our inability to observe deeper or more basic issues than those that first appear on the surface(the presenting problem in the language of employee relations counselors). For example, you think your subordinates need to listen to directions, when the deeper issue might be that you have a need to control everything. This simple reality may obscure the clarity and real sincerity of your message.

The natural response for many of us is to stereotype or label problems prematurely. The creative response demands that we keep our mind open and extend our efforts to see a new way.

For those working too hard over a long period of time on the same issues, saturation or overload can easily sneak up on their capacity to remain flexible and open to new ideas. This is a danger for "workaholics" of both sexes. The answer to that nagging problem, perched just around the bend of our imagination, may require us to leave the problem for a restful period of time. Research tells us that the brain is still working at the unconscious level, even though we aren't aware of the process.

Creativity requires a good amount of preparation and stimulation, as well as times of diversion and intellectual rest. First, **stimulate** your mind with ideas by saturating it with information. You can use techniques like brainstorming, asking twenty questions, reviewing books on the topic, using checklists, conducting interviews, traveling, writing, starting new hobbies, and listening to those around you. Second, after you have gorged yourself for a while on this information feast, just pull back, relax, and wait while you try a different activity. This is called **incubation** because we keep potentially good ideas alive and growing, like a problem baby in an incubator.

By practicing **deferring judgment or evaluation** as you let random ideas float around for a while, you will stir up creative juices and not feel as pressured to create in an unproductive way. Try to follow the intuitive logic of creativity itself. Even when resting, thinking of other things, day-dreaming or even watching television our brains are busy processing information, making connections among ideas and preparing the groundwork for more problem solving opportunities latter. Here are some **action strategies:**

Try to become more perceptive and alert to the unexpected. Don't be afraid to challenge your first perceptions and expectations; embrace ridiculous ideas for the sake of changing your angle of vision. A little playfulness and just plain foolishness is a prescription that might produce some unique thoughts. Humor can provide a sudden shift of focus and the surprise twist essential for creativity and a fresh approach to old problems.

Emotional blocks limit our ability to stretch the creative imagination and think about problems in new ways. For example, excessive commitment to our work, or winning at any cost can cause us to be perceived as a self-centered zealot. Our workers can learn the wrong lessons and become emotionally incapable of working with others and building effective workteams.

Today, the name of the game in business and almost any activity is teamwork. Our actions can teach others how to tolerate ambiguity by eliminating the excessive need for censoring the seeds of good ideas before they have an opportunity to sprout and grow. By acting consistently in a nonjudgemental manner we end up seizing opportunities to postpone evaluation for a time, while stimulating many more potentially creative ideas in our associates. The key is learning how to remain open emotionally to new opportunities and possibilities.

After we've generate as many ideas as possible through this right-brain prompting and priming, we can then evaluate their soundness, practicality, relevance and innovative potential through the process of left-brain analysis and evaluation. Effective decision making is produced through an intelligent and pragmatic integration of these two reasoning processes.

Here are some **action ideas**: Try being supportive and enthusiastic. And remember that your critical side can dominate your imagination and is affected by such emotions as the fear of failure. We need enthusiasm that builds our commitment, while downplaying perfectionism and egotism. Only you can make something good happen, so visualize your important life goals and begin to act with dedication to achieve them. Be open, take risks and feel the joy of being absorbed with new people, ideas and possibilities.

Cultural blocks can limit our creativity by constricting behavior to what is socially acceptable. People locked into their own cultural viewpoint are called ethnocentric. Cultural expectations regarding appropriate behavior can block creative exploration and expression. For example, most workers today are discouraged from any opportunity for fantasy, reflection, and playfulness. By rejecting this exploratory behavior in ourselves, we are prematurely preventing the opportunity for others to exercise their creative capacity.

Writing consultants are discovering the importance of teaching children to write using both sides of the brain. Henriette Klauser suggests that one part of our brain, the right, works for ideas, while the other, left side, works better as an editor and organizer.

Too often, writer's block results from our critical attitude, and need for instant perfection. The joy of writing is like the the playful attitude of discovery in children before they are conditioned to censor their exuberance and sense of wonder. You may have noted the relationship between this cultural block and the emotional climate discussed in the previous block; an excessively rational attitude and climate at the wrong time (this is the key, not rationality itself), can prevent the emergence of novelty, uniqueness and originality.

Here are **some action suggestions for overcoming this block.** Practice doing things your culture ignores, like spending time at work relaxing your mind, generating as many ideas as possible, and ignoring the need for any solution; unclutter your day from detail and deadlines; let your mind wander into fantasy, daydreams and general irrelevance; and consciously avoid finishing certain projects by working on a very different one when you reach a critical blockage.

Intellectual blocks to creativity occur as a result of faulty information gathering, formulation, and processing strategies. Truly creative people must balance and integrate the two primary modes of rationality; yet, some remain stuck in the emotional/intuitive realm. Individuals with preferred modes or styles of thinking about problems may display inflexible behaviors, and ignore their weaknesses.

Those with narrow intellectual skills and limited familiarity with the type of thinkers commonly found in their organization or industry, may find it difficult to prioritize issues and sort out the relevant factors in their work culture. They may need to team with other opposite types or find some way to convince others that their work or organizational culture needs a more rounded viewpoint.

In contrast, experienced and well-rounded managers and leaders quickly grasp the crucial issues at stake. They rely upon both the quantity and quality of information, and imaginatively search information for new patterns, relationships and more fruitful connections.

But, merely having information and expertise does not guarantee that ideas will be combined imaginatively. Without knowledge, imagination cannot be productive, and without imagination, even the most well-prepared minds cannot help us to perceive potentially innovative paths or entrepreneurial opportunities. Below are some **action ideas** for your consideration.

Sharpen your sense of problem assessment. Practice asking questions, and develop curiosity about how and why things go wrong more often than they might. Listen to the ideas of others, and jot down your ideas about how things can be improved. Ask questions and develop sensitivity to the problems festering below the surface. Don't always accept at face value the surface or presenting problem. Broaden or narrow the problem in order to consider a wider range of possibilities, particularly when you don't really know what you are looking for in the first place.

Formulate the real problem by asking the right questions. This reframing process is an important aspect of creativity. Be independent and courageous in your thinking. Practice extended concentration so that distractions and interruptions do not effect your ability to work anytime.

Remember, the logic of creativity tells us that good ideas can come anytime, including when we're driving or riding the subway, playing sports, listening to music, engaging in a favorite hobby, eating, sleeping travel, and talking with others about anything stimulating. Make your own list, but more importantly, workout everyday at your favorite activity and try to systematically build your creativity.

Stress is another major obstacle to creativity (see chapter6 for more discussion of stress as a self-management issue). We can define stress as the arousal of the mind-body system which, if prolonged, can fatigue or damage the human system to the point of disease. Stressors are the physical, social, and psychological conditions or situations correlated with the onset of stress.

Stress is the body's nonspecific response to any demand placed upon it, whether pleasant or unpleasant. Because the purpose of work is inherently stimulating (discounting the fact that we often destroy this inherent advantage), we should not to try to completely avoid or eliminate stress. In fact, a moderate amount of stress is necessary to facilitate any meaningful task, including work and creativity.

Different individuals have unique patterns of responding to changing work situations and stresses. Work often becomes a routine process of managing or coping with problems after they overwhelm our coping abilities. This is the reactive response. However, the preferred mode of proactively managing any change (discussed in chapter 1) is the more rewarding alternative, because we are trying to anticipate and prevent problems before they occur, or at least before they reach major crisis proportions. Which managerial stress style do you use?

Creativity begins when we learn self-regulation strategies through relaxation, in order to gain more balance and control over stress. Excessive muscle tension and worry prolongs stress, because it contributes to our failure to sustain the mental and physical rigors of thinking. Muscle tensions are actually locked into our constricted thinking patterns, and prevent us from getting outside our old, narrow perceptions and attitudes about situations and people.

Your commitment to conquering stress will produce a more positive attitude about work and other lifestyle possibilities. The resulting calming effect upon the body allows an unconscious shift of attention to more effective strategies for gathering information and putting it to the test, both in analytic or active experiencial learning endeavors.

The benefits of increased mental relaxation and concentration are more vivid imagery and enhanced perception. In addition, you will notice increased learning capabilities, higher self-esteem, and improved emotional understanding and control (a stress management technique in itself).

Here are some additional **action strategies** to help you to take charge of your stressors. Get to know your stressors and how you respond to them over time in in various situations. Determine what factors or situations seem to impact you chronically or severely. Exercise regularly and non-competitively for about three half-hour sessions a week to give you a surge of energy and increase your well-being. Eat a balanced diet because the research points increasingly towards the enormous benefits of good nutrition to our sense of physical and emotional balance.

Reexamine your life and work priorities, learn to listen actively and ask questions, and relax by creating an enlarged sense of sharing and involvement (even at work!).Allow yourself the luxury of making some mistakes, and learn to forgive others for being less than perfect. Put perfection, guilt and anger in perspective, and learn how to appreciate and celebrate success and failure, victory and defeat in more humble and constructive ways (Gutknecht and Miller1986:184-191; Gutknecht et. al., 1988: chapters 4 and 8).

The **final obstacle** to creativity is one that is not often discussed in this context: **organizational structure**. Some **organizational obstacles** include: constraints (over-control, tight deadlines), limited rewards, poor communications between units, limited boundary-spanning, and poor project management.

Organizational stimulants to creativity include: freedom to experiment, a sense of personal control, access to resources and sponsors, good project management skills, high trust, low levels of red-tape, acceptance of failure as part of the entrepreneurial process, and open communications. This book refers to these ideas in many contexts and situations.

Some **action ideas** for removing these structural blocks and supporting innovation. If you would like your organization to promote creativity and entrepreneurial innovation, then you should take responsibility for creating a performance environment where these behaviors are identified and rewarded (Farrell, 1986: 50). **First,** you should try to identify creative talent. **Second,** you need to understand how to develop, use, and reward this talent once identified. Here are some questions to ask:

1* Who are our creative people, and how do we know that they are creative?

2* What opportunities exist for creative people in our organization?

3* What barriers have we managers placed in front of creative type employees and innovative behavior?

4* In what ways do we reward creativity?

5* Do we embarrass, ridicule, and reject those workers who experiment and try new approaches?

6* How do we specifically encourage or promote experimentation and independent thinking?

7* Do you as a manager usually make all the important decisions? What types of decisions do you encourage your subordinates to make?

8* Are staff and committee meetings, round table discussions, and small group meetings always agendabound, tightly structured, timeconstricted and dominated by critical, controlorientated managers who cannot tolerate deviation or getting off the path (Sinetar, 1985).

One of the key challenges facing any organization and its leaders is how to encourage creative people to express themselves innovatively, while still maintaining the traditional culture and functions of the organization. Managers must help to reduce destructive barriers to creativity; they must change from a style of excessive control to one of effective influence; and they must learn to overcome any of their unproductive attitudes and stereotypes that result from their different generational experiences.

It is imperative that managers try to match the creative style of their subordinates to organizational needs (Wissema, VanderPol, and Messer,1980:43). In addition, the stage of a company's life cycle requires us to match the needs and capabilities of its prospective management team, with their administrative and leadership skills (Matherly and Goldsmith, 1985:11). Finally, the effective manager must match each employee's creative style to their job requirements.

For example, innovative problem solvers may be better suited to a task like creating and developing new product ideas, while others may be better suited to managing existing product lines. The most effective leaders and managers are, however, learning how to strengthen their skills in both areas. Once again, the concept of integrated or balanced thinking appears to become the most significant attribute of high achievers and performers; however, we can not expect or want all our workers to reach this level.

TECHNIQUES FOR ENHANCING CREATIVITY

The initial task here is to set the climate for exploring our creative processes and getting in touch with such aspects as imagination, intuition, and divergent thinking: the attitudes, beliefs, expectations, abilities, interests, thinking styles and anything that will put you in a more receptive and self-aware frame of mind.

Whatever we try, the goal when trying to promote creativity is to get out of our critical, analytical left-brain for the moment. Remember, we are ultimately interested in using both sides of the brain and associated processes.

BE RECEPTIVE TO NEW AND PROXIMATE IDEAS

The key is learning how see connections within data that does not appear at first blush to contain relevant information to your task. Acquiring data is only the first stage of our task because we are most interested in moving to those ideas that can truly make a difference.

We need to become more aware of excessive criticism in the early stage of generating ideas. Just because we've often been taught at school and conditioned at work to evaluate ideas, doesn't mean we can't decide upon the best times and places to critically evaluate. Each of us must learn to suspend our critical capabilities when we're trying to generate creative ideas and alternatives.

In addition, we must push beyond the linear, logical limits of the immediately relevant to the more fuzzy boundaries of the only approximately relevant. This is because reasoning with analogies (approximately relevant) enables individuals to work on problems without feeling the stress of practicality, the intimidating eye of relevancy, or the fear of our internal censor.

Being receptive means challenging old thinking habits, reflecting about obstacles to creative processes, and not getting bogged down trying to work with only bits and pieces that must logically resemble the topic or problem. It also means patiently getting into new situations in the world and listening, observing, and risking with a non-judgmental attitude. Creative people are obviously in touch with themselves and open to any new strategies that might produce insights, connections, and imaginative solutions to personal and organizational problems.

USE CHECKLISTS

Osborne (1963) offers the idea of getting a list of topics or words and consider them in light of the key topics or subjects about which you're trying to generate some creative angles. The list could include any of the following :

> *Adapt? Put to other uses? New ways to use as is? Other uses if modified? What else is like this? What other ideas does this suggest?

> *Modify? New style? Change meaning, color, motion, sound, odor form, shape? Other changes?

*Magnify? What to add? More time? Greater frequency? Stronger? Higher? Longer? Thicker? Extra value? Duplicate?

*Minify? What to subtract? Smaller? Condensed? Miniature? Lower?

*Substitute? Who else instead? What else instead? Other ingredients? Other materials? Other processes, powers, places, approaches?

*Rearrange? Interchange components? Other pattern, layout, sequence? Transpose cause and effect? Change pace? Change schedule?

*Reverse? Transpose positive and negative? How about opposites? Turn it backwards? Turn it upside down? Reverse roles?

*Combine? How about a blend, an alloy, an assortment, an ensemble? Combine units, purposes, appeals, ideas?

INCUBATE IDEAS

This strategy is to establish the proper conditions for making new or unexpected connections. Try to immerse yourself in a situation, issue or condition; daydream, play music, exert yourself to your limits, as you wait for revelations, connections, and implications. Patience and timing are key virtues here, and their diligent cultivation will produce creative results.

Now back off and change directions by doing the opposite and let data and ideas mix in the stew bellow the level of awareness. Read anything to stimulate your imagination. Don't expect some grand illumination, just be aware of less dramatic insights and connections, which can be constantly built upon.

Remember, waiting for great leaps of imagination can place excessive stress and performance pressure on you; be patient, avoid procrastination, and enthusiastically establish a firm foundation gathering information and practicing your idea generating strategies everyday. Accept the fact that the kernel of all new ideas lies in the process of building upon the best of the past. We can actively learn anytime by modifying, borrowing, combining, synthesizing, evaluating and recognizing the fertile, historical soil of former innovations or inventions.

LISTING ATTRIBUTES

Crawford (1954) first developed this technique for stimulating creativity. The process is a special type of of checklist that asks you to list all the attributes of the product, idea, situation, or problem. Next, take each attribute and probe it, as it contains some essence and possible clue about the creative potential of the product, idea, or service change under consideration.

For example, after listing the attributes of an effective team or group, one then evaluates each attribute separately in order to improve upon the idea. If we stated that work groups require cohesiveness, goals, norms, leadership, interaction, and roles, then we might focus on just one attribute in order to improve them.

Let's take group cohesiveness as the attribute that we are going to analyze in order to improve work groups. We might begin with a definition of what cohesiveness is: the characteristics of the group in which the forces acting on the group members to remain and participate are greater than those acting on members to leave it (Gutknecht and Miller,1986:144). Using this definition as a starting point, how could we improve the process of building group cohesiveness?

Let me suggest several possibilities from my own brainstorming of alternatives derived from the above definition. Establish common interests and participate in extracurricular activities together in order to improve the chances of agreeing on important group goals to work toward. Increase the frequency of positive interaction and informal visiting and interaction at the worksite. Introduce some type of intergroup competition because groups will increase cohesiveness when they identify a common enemy. And finally, hire people with similar characteristics because they will function more like us and probably support our group goals. The basic idea behind this generating lists technique is to probe each component and ask, "How can this be done differently or viewed from a more productive angle."

FORCING RELATIONSHIPS

The idea here is to force a relationship between two previously unrelated things, concepts, or products. The forced relationship is established using such items as catalogs, magazines, books, or dictionaries, and selecting an ides or subject of interest for new possible combinations.

Next, the second word or subject is also mechanically selected, and the two elements are considered together to evoke original thoughts derived from the forced associations. The process is really to force associations between the old and the new, the mundane and the extraordinary; what you know and what you need to speculate about.

ALTERNATION PRINCIPLES: THINKING-JUDGING, SOLO-TEAM, INVOLVE-DETACH

Thinking-Judging is the principle that suggests we generate ideas first and then judge them. Thinking for increasing our creative output requires that we record every idea, whether good or bad, without initially judging or evaluating them.

Ideas themselves become the stimulus for other ideas. By giving our ideas the green light, our mind begins to move faster, rapidly generating new ideas without slowing down for fear of obstacles or detours ahead. Associations spring to life more fluidly and naturally. This process of free association taps the deeper sources of the unconscious for embedded ideas by avoiding internal censors, like low self-esteem and the fear of failure.

The factors of judgment and critical evaluation are not forgotten but only postponed. Deferring judgment has also been called divergent or lateral thinking (DeBono, 1967). Lateral thinking helps us challenge assumptions in ways that logical thinking does not. This occurs as the mind interrupts its habitual, organized thought process and leaps "sideways" out of its ingrained patterns. When this happens, the brain often links unrelated cognitive and neural patterns and synaptic connections, helping us to see problems in new ways. Any time you find yourself reacting to an idea as it seems to float into awareness, just jot it down.

Lynch (1984:102-105) has given us some interesting insights regarding another important technique that utilizes the divergent thinking process, brainstorming. This long available technique was first practiced in India as part of a Hindu religious ceremony called Prai-Barshana, which means *"outside yourself questioning"*.

The method is first formally identified by Alex Osborn in 1938 as **brainstorming**. It became the technique for using the brain's capabilities for intuitive insight in the right hemisphere to storm elements of a more creative approach to solving problems. A more formal definition is the uninhibited development of ideas, suggestions, and insights by individuals or groups.

The first thing we need to remember is to suspend our judgmental attitudes and critical, left-brained censor. Be prepared to record all ideas generated without evaluating their relevance, usefulness or validity. Watch for nonverbal put-downs such as a snicker, rolling eyes, or condescending humor; and verbal put-downs such as "that will never work" or "top management will never approve of that." Remember, you are trying to suspend your preconceived ideas and generate as many ideas as possible over a short, fixed time span; evaluation will come at a later stage in the process.

Brainstorming builds upon the process of free-association of ideas so each person should express their ideas whenever they spring to awareness. Others ideas will often serve as a stimulus to your own ideas. Let's now review the stages of brainstorming.

1. FREE WHEEL- Generate as many ideas as possible on a topic, problem, situation or attribute. The ideas should not be criticized or evaluated. Set an initial time limit of approximately THIRTY minutes.

2. RECORD--The ideas generated should be recorded on a chalk board or notebook.

3. REST AND INCUBATION- About halfway through the time frame ask participants to close their eyes, fold their arms in a relaxed way, and rest their heads. Suggest that they reflect uncritically on the ideas already generated.

4. RESUME FREEWHEELING--The group recorder (who may also be the group leader) can now resume the recording the ideas as they are generated during the remaining FIFTEEN minutes. The leader-recorder should try to facilitate not directly control or dominate the free association process and remind the participants of the rules.

5. COMBINE AND EVALUATE--After the ideas have been generated and recorded the group should then try to combine, categorize, or organize the ideas produced. Here the facilitator can direct a discussion and evaluation about the ideas listed. Participants can add more ideas. Through these discussions the scope of the situation or problem can be clarified, and possible solutions generated.

6. RETURN TO FREE WHEEL--You can return to the free wheel brainstorming of ideas if at any time the group decides to expand upon one key idea or solution.

Solo/team alternation of effort suggests that some people work better together as individuals, while others improve their work when they join a team or group effort. However, for the type of complex problems that most individuals and organizations are facing today, the advantages of pooling one's resources, talent, knowledge, and expertise is obvious. Even groups can benefit by giving individuals assigned work alone, away from the group. Even entrepreneurs improve the quality of their ideas after participating in groups.

The alternating principle of **involvement/detachment** is a psychological dimension of the last idea. Sometimes we need to not only leave a problem by departing a group or leaving our office; we also need to depart consciously. People often get so overloaded, hung-up, burned-out, frustrated and intense that they need a mental, emotional and physical break.

Relaxation and rest away from any situation can provide needed time for perspective, humility, and just the opportunity to gain renewed enthusiasm, optimism and faith in one's own abilities. Also, we find that the obstacles that formerly blocked our creativity diminish when our attention is focused away from the need to quickly produce insights.

CONCLUSIONS

Creativity is the ability to produce something of innovative beauty through imaginative skill. Most workers can learn to use a rich variety of creativity enhancement strategies with versatility and skill. However, managers and all employees must continue to nurture this aesthetic and practical process in all aspects of their work and personal lives.

We must all learn the active learning lesson of the three attributes of the creative process: sensitivity to problems often overlooked by others; fluency in generating ideas when faced with difficult situations problems; and finally, flexibility to examine many alternatives and to determine the most beneficial and innovative outcomes.

Creative leaders, managers, and workers can work together to help establish creative organizations. They can support a climate for innovation to flourish and go to a great deal of trouble to find creative people. Channels of communication must be open and information shared.

One essential for a company's long-term survival is the ability to manage the challenges of change and proactively master new competitive situations. Managing change is such an important skill because it requires modifications and significant departures from the organizations established operations and procedures. Most managers can improve their general performance by understanding at least some principles of creativity.

The truly creative firm is one where both innovative and adaptive behavior are nurtured, supported, and rewarded. By recognizing the potential contributions from both styles of management, organizations can build more balanced, creative management teams which can ultimately enhance the organization's effectiveness (Matherly and Goldsmith, 1985: 11).

The bottom line is that productive management supports organizational practices that express creativity as a way of organizational life, and every employee can use some creative techniques to aspire to become more effective. Here are some *action strategies* for igniting the creative sparks in any organization.

Finds ways to constantly link all levels of the organization together. This means valuing creativity and innovation because the success of any enterprise is tied to its quality of people and their ideas and skills. Build a culture of accomplishment, experimentation and pride in innovation through these creative interchanges. This type of organization is quick to give credit for creative behavior in order to sustain a climate of excellence through innovation.

Workers need to feel wanted, appreciated, and successful. Innovative organizations get excited about the challenges ahead, about ideas, concepts, people and products, regardless of the difficulties encountered. They recognize that down-cycles are inevitable, but success over the long-term is their goal.

Such organizations don't often interfere in the creative process. They respect their employees' ability to develop, plan, evaluate, and implement innovative and potentially productive ideas and projects. Such organizations are quite demanding and only support an environment that supports the best possible outcomes, given the current conditions, personnel, and resources. They appreciate mistakes because they know that only in such an open and experimental climate can creativity and productive innovation occur.

Personnel in innovative organizations listen with their heads and their hearts. Creative and entrepreneurial people need responsive and probing managers to bounce their ideas off, to put things in practical perspective and to mobilize resources and supports for their best ideas and products.

There is creative potential in virtually all of us, although it emerges from deep within and shows itself in different ways. Let's get on with important work and eliminate the excuses that block our path and traps us in creative immaturity. While we whimper that we are not capable enough to sustain that which is reserved for some artistic elite, the everyday world is banging at our door.

5

SELF-MANAGEMENT, PART 1: MANAGING BEHAVIOR, TIME AND OTHER PRIORITIES

INTRODUCTION

This chapter explores the skills of self-management, managing behavior, personal growth and awareness skills. We examine what organizinging means as a strategy that links individual success with system concerns, the relevance of self-esteem for managing people and developing human resources, and the importance of understanding how to prioritize and achieve our goals through time management and proven behavioral change methods. Other self-management topics and strategies like individual health promotion and stress will be discussed in chapter 6.

Workers today are more educated and aware than ever before of changing trends around them. They also indicate the desire to become involved, participate more actively and contribute more productively to their careers and organizations. Employees at all organizational levels need to feel in control to make meaningful and responsible choices which integrate personal needs with valued organizational missions and goals. Indeed, issues of control become even more important to employees when their ability to influence personal or work situations is lacking.   Here feelings of victimization can encourage status-quo thinking, and the resistance to change.

How can we improve our ability to become more aware and sensitive to the effects of change on others, the stresses around us, the consequences of flawed personal decision making, the often destructive way we define and use power and control strategies, and the impacts that our personal handling of transitions exert upon our employees and organizations? We must always begin with each individual's awareness, skill, knowledge and responsibility levels.

Let's explore for a moment, the last dimension just listed, responsibility. Personal responsibility is such an important aspect of any individual's ability to lead or manage effectively. The responsible leader has placed the power and control issues in proper perspective, and never passes problems upstream or downstream without making suggestions for their solution.

This professional also has good self-esteem or that deep feeling of worth and value that supports both empathy and a probing attitude. The idea of self-worth is based upon self-awareness, a positive self-image, and good self acceptance. Self image is built upon the subjective perception of our strengths and weaknesses, indicating how we accept ourselves: either through positive feelings of confidence, or negative feelings of deficiency, insecurity and lack of self-confidence in our abilities, potentials and skills.

One indication of good self-esteem is acceptance of work as a life-long learning adventure, full of marvelous opportunities and surprises. Probably more than any one attitude, the ability to draw lessons from failure is the key difference between those who succeed and those who become "failures."

Leaders and employees with good self-esteem seldom waste time choosing the wrong measures and means for comparing themselves; they already know they possess value for themselves and desire to give even more of their time and energy to helping others to succeed. Their standards for comparison derive from within and pertain to career performance, not meaningless personal status contests.

What does a damaged sense of self-esteem look like in the workplace? The *self-depreciating doormat type* is easy for most people to recognize, due to their need to please everyone and their failure to be assertive. The *habitual conflict prone employee* often starts a ruckus because they have low self-esteem and must displace their feelings of low self-worth through the attack upon others ideas and projects. A bit more subtle type is the *overachiever-controlle*r who can't ask questions, won't admit errors, has a difficult time participating and can't delegate effectively.

The message for those concerned with improving their self-management is that each individual's level of self-esteem is not determined, in fact, (although it is correlated with these variables) by race, sex, religion, or class standing. Instead, self-worth often comes from the power of the mind and our ability to learn skills such as assessing, evaluating, motivating, communicating, planning, coordinating, leading, participating with and caring for others.

Learning these proactive, self-management skills requires only two key commitments. First, that we become absolutely honest with ourselves. Many fear what a rigorous search will yield. Second, we must try to identify and build upon those abilities and strengths in order to reduce our limitations. With honesty and the proper perspective for planning and skill building, we will more likely achieve consistent and meaningful development for ourselves and organizations.

ORGANIZING AS PERSONAL STRATEGY

Organizing is making arrangements that facilitate personal and system wide meaning and purpose. This linkage is important as we discovered in chapter 2. Since humans have a natural desire to do meaningful things, whether at work or play, they are always busy organizing the seven essentials : tasks, information, activities, people, capital, technology, spatial environments, etc. In fact, the state of our health and well-being is often related to our skillful organizing, controlling planning, motivating, goal setting and managing priorities; the means through which we organize and make sense of our work and personal lives.

These techniques facilitate the creation of meaning structures that bring together interdependent actions into sequences of activity, whether individual, or as part of a larger system (see chapter 2). Organizing at the individual level is composed of those self-management activities that link personal and organizationally relevant values, assumptions, interests, needs and behaviors into larger efforts.

By organizing, we also create meaning, balance and consistency in our lives. We then can accomplish important goals and objectives because through linking our organizing activities together, we have increased our leverage to make more effective use of the interdependent resources provided by larger systems.

However, some types of organizing, as either process or function, are helpful, effective and productive; and other types of organizing are dysfunctional, unproductive and ineffective. Functional systems make sense to people because they are balanced and link together important values, goals and tasks to create quality products and services for clients, employees, customers and stakeholder.

Good self-managers always know two things. First they know themselves and are open to new information for growth. Second, they know that all organizing activities are linked at different levels, whether personal, work or social. Thus, our keys to success are really the strategies and techniques for organizing and helping everyone to work together more effectively and productively.

Self-management does not mean that we can then be right all the time, or always win through intimidation (a short-run strategy). But more importantly, it requires us to learn how to design effective systems for the long-term development of both human and capital resources.

Healthy and effective employees know what helps to create meaning, even though they sometimes don't act like it. First, people need to know the reasons why various organizing arrangements (whether work responsibilities, family curfew, or organizational structure) have been chosen. Second, they need to feel involved and participate in some way designing these arrangements. Third, they need to feel that these arrangements will actually facilitate their achievements (not unearned gifts) of personal goals, work success and meaningful, diverse rewards.

It is almost impossible to organize and manage our personal lives without some assistance from the organizing activity going on within our work and organizations, and the patterns of organizing occurring outside the organization (of family, neighborhood, community, region, nation and today, world)

Two questions are important here. First, are the purposes that are promoted by this system ones that I can believe in and work toward? Second, is this system a well organized and an effective use of my time?

To really answer these two questions you need to know your own priorities, values, needs, interests, and wants. What is really important to you and does this system (job, family, religion, program, club, organization) help me to achieve it?

In addition, you must clearly examine what you are currently doing. Ask yourself how you spend your time, and if you are aware of things that might detract you from actually accomplishing what you desire, love, need, and value. Remember the following **action suggestion**:

Keep a log and list both your goals and your actual behaviors-activities. Then every week or month, note any discrepancies between them. If you find many discrepancies, you are possibly not effectively organizing your life very well in that area of life that you are working upon. Then decisions must be made. You might choose to adjust either your values, interest, or goals. You could choose to change behaviors, or leave an unproductive situation. Finally, you might try to convince others that it is okay to work toward divergent goals, or even try changing the incompatible system itself.

HEALTH PROMOTION AND PERSONAL BEHAVIOR CHANGE

Our concern in this section of the chapter is helping individuals to change their negative habits and behaviors, including those that impact our health and its costs to our organization and society. We will explore behavioral change strategies adopted from research on motivation, goal setting, affirmations, rewards, self-esteem, time management, and assertiveness.

In order to meet system-wide goals, the organization must sponsor programs that effectively encourage positive, skill development and behavioral changes. Any program that you design must take into consideration how people learn to change negative behavior and ineffective work patterns.

Personal development and learning activities (also discussed in chapter 3), including those focused upon health promotion, should emphasize three aspects of change: **assessment**--evaluating, taking stock of your life; **interventions**--finding methods, practices, and techniques that work for you or the organization; and **planning**--trying actions that when properly followed, actually lead to success. Let's return to the topic of personal health promotion.

HEALTH PROMOTION AND THE INDIVIDUAL

In chapter 7 we will discuss four levels of organizational health promotion. Here let's briefly discuss the stages because they have equivalent linkages to the individual level. The first level is focused upon building **awareness and information** through introductory talks about health promotion or payroll stuffers on changing negative health behaviors.

The second level is general health **information**, along with structured programs, i.e., hypertension control screenings and Health Risk Appraisals (HRA). These programs serve to determine risk factors which predispose us to disease. This motivational level begins to consolidate some of the information gained through awareness and utilize it to assess and make behavioral change more relevant and likely.

The third level is composed of fairly **comprehensive health promotion programs** that focus upon **intervention systems for ongoing behavioral change.** These programs include workshops on a variety of health and wellness topics. This level also includes opportunities for promoting personal development through human resource incentives, rewards and supporting policies.

The fourth level is concerned with **organizational change.** This level contains programs that address the full range of structural and leadership issues. The topics of concern are organizational work redesign, cultural change, organizational philosophy, values, norms, and management styles.

Any training program or program for behavioral change can build upon this information. We can also observe that personal development can be encouraged and supported by organizational actions, policies, and changes. For example, information and assessment (taking programs), personal planning (with the assistance of organizational policies, incentives, and rewards) and taking action (supported by the organizational culture and structure) are linked in any effective change program or strategy.

We are also trying to get each individual to think more about those unproductive behaviors, whether work or lifestyle, over which they can exert some control. Our goal is to get individuals to: (1) recognize their personal responsibility for assessing their behaviors; (2) use reliable interventions; (3) plan to change negative behaviors (see chapter 6 for review); and (4) practice the recommended new behaviors to the best of their ability and encourage the organization to develop supports, policies and reward structures.

FACILITATING BEHAVIORAL CHANGE

Much organizational behavior research has attempted to explain the conceptual reasons why people practice healthy/unhealthy work. They have not done as well telling leaders and managers how to build programs that motivate people to change.
Our discussion in this chapter will only provide a brief overview of a

Our discussion in this chapter will only provide a brief overview of a complex topic and then move on to some specifics. Once again we will use the example of health promotion but these ideas have relevance for any change or program development strategy.

There are two key reasons why employees practice healthy or unhealthy (effective or ineffective) behavior. One is the degree to which a person **perceives** a benefit or threat. This is influenced by general values (interest and concerns), specific beliefs and beliefs about the seriousness of a situation or problem to the individual (consequences). The second factor relates to **perception that adopting a particular behavioral change will be effective** in reducing the personal threat/potential problem (or its cost in money, time, sacrifice of lifestyle pleasures) mentioned in the first reason.

Taking the health promotion example, these beliefs have been shown to impact health habits of the man or woman who feels vulnerable to a stroke and is considering dietary changes or the need to better monitor their blood pressure. They may believe that heredity is destiny and that dietary changes alone will not help much to reduce their risk. Also, he/she enjoys eating high fat gourmet foods and believes that changing these practices would reduce this pleasure of eating exotic foods. Although the belief in personal vulnerability is high, his/her confidence that diet alone will be effective or is worth the personal cost, will probably make any major lifestyle changes difficult.

The process of behavior change for positive work and health/lifestyle habits begins with some perspective or information that makes the prospects of behavioral change at least intriguing, interesting, or meaningful. Individuals must try to make the connection between behaviors and positive functioning (wellness), more real, relevant and necessary. This link must also be established in any change, training or development program workshop, seminar, lecture. The focus is upon those factors and risks that the individual has some control over.

Next, the individual must find the motivation and opportunity to acquire new assessment skills and knowledge that lead to more personally useful and productive results (I tried that technique and it seems to make a difference). This process further personalizes the link between behavior and health, as the individual begins to see that changes in certain areas of their work or personal life have positive impacts on other life dimensions.

Some individuals can begin at an early stage to feel more confident about defining health risks and defining modifiable behaviors (we can personally change and control these lifestyle risk factors-smoking, weight, diet, exercise, stress) versus *unmodifiable factors, like* heredity, unhealthy environment, which the individual has much less direct control over. And finally, people need to broaden their involvements, find support (friends, colleagues, family, boss) and begin to plan (based upon abilities and interests) to find the motivation, and take specific actions to change behaviors.

Of course, many activities can provide much relevant foundational knowledge to begin the process. But the choices and decision to plan priorities and act effectively for oneself, one's career, and one's organization, must eventually become your decision.

MOTIVATION: HOW TO BUILD AND SUSTAIN IT
UNTIL YOU REACH YOUR GOAL

CHECK [/] THE STATEMENTS BELOW THAT ACCURATELY REFLECTS YOUR MOTIVATIONAL LEVEL AT THIS TIME.

[ ] 1.When I begin programs or regimens to change my behavior (like poor performance, being late to work, improving exercise patterns or diet) I hear the music of "The Rocky Theme" but this tune turns to "Taps" by dusk of the 10th day.

[ ] 2. I have been known to reward myself for being "good" (writing that book I know I can write or staying on my diet) by being "bad" (procrastinating or asking for one more orders of fries).

[ ] 3. The last time I successfully "made" a goal, I was playing basketball.

[ ] 4. It's easy for me to think positive--until it looks like things could possibly go wrong.

[ ] 5. I can stay motivated until I stop and think about what it is I must accomplish. Then I do something dumb (lose my temper, forget to attend the seminar I signed up for, raid the refrigerator) and try to forget.

THE STATEMENTS BELOW ARE CHARACTERISTIC OF A PERSON WHO IS HIGHLY MOTIVATED. CHECK [/] THE ONES WHICH APPLY TO YOU AT THIS TIME.

[ ] 1. I frequently review the goals I have set for long-term behavioral change (no quality defects for my unit, creating a prestigious college program, improving weight control).

[ ] 2. I reward myself for small successes that keep me inching toward my goals. I know that the foundation for building anything lies in mastering the building blocks with enthusiasm, perseverance and a commitment to quality.

[ ] 3. I frequently visualize myself in the future reaping the rewards for successfully achieving my goals.

[ ] 4. I no longer have high peaks and deep valleys in my motivation. I can sustain a level of quiet confidence because I know where I am going and how I am going to get there.

[ ] 5. I dwell on and affirm the things that I value and am no longer fearful or anxious that the things I don't desire or support will come to pass. I don't dwell upon negative thoughts. However, I am receptive to feedback and know that I can learn a great deal from my mistakes.

Take heart if you could not check all of these statements at this time. When you have had an opportunity to implement some of the ideas and techniques chances are good you will fare much better.

WHAT IS POSITIVE SELF-MOTIVATION?

Positive self-motivation as it applies to the solution to a behavior/health problem can best be seen as a learned skill. Unlike the common perception of motivation as a force which acts on us from without, true self-motivation is developed from within through the application of specific, definable techniques. It's a sustained energy and belief that you can accomplish your desired objectives, regardless of the odds. Your friend's or spouse's desire for you to change get a raise or promotion or lose weight) is not alone enough to motivate you toward that end. You must recognize the need to change, improve and desire to do whatever is necessary to get the job done.

WHAT KIND OF PLAN DO I NEED TO BE SUCCESSFUL?

By enrolling in a training and development, behavioral change, or health promotion program, I assume you have certain energy or disposition to improve and have beliefs about maximizing your effectiveness, what it takes to get a promotion, or why wellness requires you to change various lifestyle habits. We have already explained that this process does not call for quick fix solutions, therefore, your chances of long term success are very good.

It is entirely possible that you were highly motivated when you started your last attempt at behavioral change (stopping your destructive arguing, improving your diet, start exercising, stop smoking, no more procrastinating). But behavior change requires good information.

For example, there is no greater exercise in willpower than that shown by dieters who have cut their calories drastically. However, the evidence also suggests that people who constantly start and stop diets will actually gain weight more readily. So, the first thing to understand about motivation is that all the right kind of it in the world will not help you if you do not have the right information and plan to effectively how to use it.

Also, all the information in the world will do you no good if you are not motivated or energized to act. Information, motivation and planning must go together. The first step then is to introduce you to some simple techniques that will help you build and sustain positive self-motivation. For many people who are seeking to gain control over a behavioral, work or health concern, the ability to build and sustain their motivation toward a worthwhile goal is the difference between a glowing success and a frustrating failure.

1. After you have determined what you want, the next step is to set some written goals that clearly state what you expect to achieve in the short, medium, and long term.

2. You next need to develop mental pictures of yourself achieving these goals and reaping the rewards that accompany success. This includes the development of mental images of yourself that are compatible with a person who is successful. We will help you do this in two ways; through self-visualization and through a process known as affirmation.

3. You need to become a "doer" who is not concerned with perfection, and who sees "failures" (there is really no such thing) as important learning experiences; the kind of person who realizes that there are many steps leading to the final destination. As long as you are making progress, whether measured in "inches" or miles, you are moving closer to your goals. This is important because motivation is sustained by seeing and feeling progress.

For example, during the first 10 days to two weeks of eating low-calorie foods, dieters can easily see the results on their scales. Despite feeling deprived, they can usually hang in there because their weight is consistently dropping. (If it isn't, they may not last even 10 days.) But what happens when the weight loss stops or slows to a snail's pace? They have only one way to measure progress and when it fails, they become quickly demoralized and unable to continue.

4. Finally, you need to plan how you will tangibly reward yourself when you accomplish the steps leading to your ultimate goal; giving yourself credit for small as well as big successes.

GOALS: WHAT KIND SHOULD I SET ?

The goals you set for any behavioral change program and anything else you want to accomplish in life should satisfy the following criteria. Although we have already alluded to this topic in other chapters, let's review just in case you are reading only this chapter. Goals should be:

1. **Specific**--Goals need to zero in on exactly what it is you want by answering the questions: where, and how, and what.

2. **Time-limited**--Your goals must be brought into the here and now by setting some time limits for their resolution.

3. **Possible**--In their enthusiasm to accomplish a lot quickly, many people are tempted to set a goal like losing too much weight in too little time. Be realistic and remind yourself that remaining at normal weight without a constant struggle should be the long-term objective.

Here is a prototype for how you may want to set some specific goals for yourself. Notice these three goals answer the questions where, how, and what. Write your variations of these suggested goals in the space provided if you wish . (Note that we have written these goals as affirmations as though they have already occurred. This affirmation principle is discussed below). We will continue to focus upon the weight example here but you may substitute any work, in-terpersonal, or health behavior that you have assessed as needing some positive change.

1. **WHERE do I want to go?** (My long term goal)
EX. I comfortably maintain _____ pounds by practicing good eating

and lifestyle habits found in this program.

GOALS

_____

_____

_____

_____

2. HOW am I going to get there? (My intermediate goal).
EX. Having identified the lifestyle habits important to my success, I am practicing to make them completely automatic.

GOALS

_____

_____

_____

_____

3. WHAT am I going to do first (next)? (My immediate goal)
EX. I am in control of my food intake and energy output now!

GOALS

_____

_____

_____

_____

HOW TO CONTROL YOUR TIME

Poor time management can cause stress, frustration, and lowered self-esteem which in turn can produce inactivity, stress, poor work performance, bad nutrition and overeating. Additionally, many people seeking a solution to their problems feel they must lower the priority they have placed on changing that particular behavior in order to be successful. The exact opposite is more often true. Failure to plan behavioral change situations and to allow proper time for your goal attainment is a frequently occurring problem .

The material in this section will help you analyze your time utilization, set some time management goals, and provide techniques for improving the way you use your time in order to change bad health habits.

BELOW ARE SEVEN STATEMENTS, EACH REPRESENTING A COMMON SYMPTOM OF POOR TIME MANAGEMENT. CHECK [/] THE ONES THAT APPLY TO YOU.

[ ] 1. When I am faced with a difficult decision with equally unpleasant alternatives, I decisively flip a coin, and then I flip it again, and then again,.and then again...

[ ] 2. I frequently experience fatigue and am non-productive for long stretches of time, but boy, you should see me on Friday at 3 o'clock.

[ ] 3. I find myself rushing to accomplish the things I feel are important so I can spend my precious time on the unimportant things.

[ ] 4. If I ever got the time to do what I wanted to do, I'd probably have a hard time figuring out what I wanted to do.

[ ] 5. The tag team of Details and Demands have a stranglehold on my life.

[ ] 6. Whenever deadlines and I meet, I usually get beat.

[ ] 7. Not only are the rats winning the race, I'm about to get lapped.

If you consistently experience any of these, you could no doubt benefit from improved time management.

THE FOLLOWING ITEMS RELATE SPECIFICALLY TO THE IMPORTANCE OF MANAGING TIME. FOR EACH INDIVIDUAL) CHECK [/] THE ONES THAT APPLY TO YOU.

[ ] **1.** The combined hours in a day I spend thinking about and eating food is equal to all my waking hours plus 4.

[ ] **2.** I rarely take the time to sit down and relax.

[ ] **3.** If I keep busy and don't schedule time to exercise, I'll probably feel better.

[ ] **4.** My feeling of contentment or stress tells me when it is time to light-up or pig-out.

[ ] **5.** The feeling that there is too much to do in too little time frequently causes me to experience stress. When this happens I either smoke, pour a drink, watch T.V. or eat (often all at the same time).

If you checked one or more of the above, you are now probably aware of the importance of managing your time better for lasting success in changing your behavior.

Q: DOESN'T BEING HIGHLY ORGANIZED AND EFFICIENT MEAN A LOSS OF SPONTANEITY TOWARD LIFE AND BEHAVING LIKE A ROBOT?

A: No. Control of your time (and your life) does not mean becoming super-organized, super-busy, or preoccupied with every moment of your day as it slips by. Good time management allows you to be flexible and spontaneous. Too much organization is as ineffective as too little. Learning to manage your time effectively will not take away your individuality and freedom.

Q: I WASTE LOTS OF TIME TRYING TO MAKE DECISIONS. WHAT CAN I DO ABOUT IT?

First, understand some of the original decisions you may have made long ago that may have helped produced this indecisiveness. We can think of these decisions as habits of thought that when practiced over time, become difficult to break away from. Dr. Harold Greenwald in his book, **Direct Decision Therapy**, indicates there are at least eight of these (Gutknecht, et. al., 1988).

Check any that may apply to you:

[ ] **1.** I don't want to hurt anyone

[ ] **2.** Everything I do must be easy.

[ ] **3.** Nothing that I do should be easy, instead everything should be hard.

[ ] **4.** I never want to become really tired, or work too hard.

[ ] **5.** I want to suffer as little pain as I possibly can.

[ ] **6.** I want to liked by everyone.

[ ] **7.** If I experience too much pleasure, I may be punished.

[ ] **8.** I should never feel guilty or angry.

Here are some of the ideas Dr. Greenwald suggests for helping you overcome some of the above stated decisions that keep you from acting decisively:

1. State in writing the decision you are having trouble making and the conflicting feelings you have regarding this decision.

2. Determine the original decision that is causing the conflict.

3. What other decisions do you have available to you besides the one you usually make?

4. Decide on a new alternative, write it down, and put it into practice.

5. Reward yourself each time you make this new decision.
Listed below are the three self-defeating statements given by Albert

Ellis and William Knaus (**Overcoming Procrastination**) as the cause of most procrastination (Gutknecht, et. al., 1988).

1. "I must receive acclaim for things that I accomplish. If I don't, I might as well put off the difficult tasks."

2. "The world must give me the things I want without me giving anything in return or suffering deprivation. Until it does, I'll put off future gain for present ease."

3. "Everyone must treat me fairly and kindly. If they don't, I'll spite them by goofing off even though in the process I will be hurting myself more than anyone."

These attitudes are acquired from our environment as we grow up and are chiefly the result of a low tolerance to frustration. We view a task as difficult and we delay it because we tell ourselves, consciously or subconsciously, that we will benefit more than if we were to complete it. Ellis and Knaus describe many different ways to overcome procrastination; here are action techniques they mention as useful in dealing with this problem:

(Place a check [/] next to the techniques that you feel will help you start and finish difficult tasks on time.)

[ ] **1.** Reward yourself upon immediate completion of of a task you have been delaying.

[ ] **2.** You can penalize yourself by doing something you don't like immediately after you procrastinate.

[ ] **3.** Jog your memory by using written reminders. Instead of simply listing a task urgently needed to be accomplished, write a motivating statement that will inspire you to act. Perhaps write the reward you will give yourself for completing this job on time.

[ ] **4.** Since procrastinators have the tendency to let tasks pile up until they have dozens of them all pressing to get done, decide to

tackle one (the most urgent one) for a predesignated amount of time. Don't tell yourself you must do it all at one time. When your time is up, you may just surprise yourself by wanting to continue. Set yourself another time goal and continue. Always allow yourself the chance to end your work and come back to it later.

[ ] 5. When you are working on a task you enjoy, you may find it easy to switch to another related task that you've been putting off. If you're already in the kitchen baking something for your family, you could probably find time to clean the refrigerator.

[ ] 6. Another useful strategy is to do something the minute you think of it. Our attention span is short and if we choose to put off even a small task, we can be faced with a mountain of small things to do at a later time.

[ ] 7. Establish a routine or a time schedule for mundane work that tends to pile up. An example of this given in **Overcoming Procrastination** is the development of a consistent exercise schedule. If you schedule your exercise regimen first thing in the morning and stick to it, you will form a habit that before long you will miss if it is not there. Not incidentally, the positive payoff you will receive from exercising the way we have earlier recommended, will be reason enough to keep you going.

[ ] 8. Provide yourself with an environment that is conducive to starting and completing the task at hand. Physically remove, if necessary, the distractions in your work or study area such as your stereo, radio, or TV to provide an atmosphere that will not divert you from the job at hand.

[ ] 9. Use a friend or acquaintance to help you complete a task you may have trouble completing but the other person doesn't. This may help for the following reasons: 1) You will be motivated to complete the task because you will not want to inconvenience your friend; 2) Difficult activities don't seem as hard when you are doing them with someone else; 3) If you have been afraid of failing at this task, you will find safety in numbers. Having this person to help you will

probably increase your chance for success.

[ ]10. Don't expect to be perfect from the start. Look for overall improvement and not an immediate solution to your procrastination problem.

Q: HOW CAN I DETERMINE WHAT IS IMPORTANT AND UNIMPORTANT TO ME SO I WILL KNOW HOW BEST TO USE MY TIME?

A: You will need to establish priorities for your life right now. These priorities may change in 6 months or a year but you will need to set goals for your life or time management won't have any relevance to you. Here are some reasons you need these goals:

1. To help you discover what you really want to do.
2. To help motivate you to do it.
3. To give meaning to the way you spend your time.
4. To give you a direction and help you feel in control of your destiny.
5. To reduce unnecessary conflict over how to use your time.
6. To save time.

HOW TO SET PRIORITIES FOR YOUR LIFE

In the space below, write your goals. Although, we have already discussed this topic, here is another good opportunity to review your priorities and note any changes in your understanding of them.

Remember from our motivation discussion earlier that a good personal goal plan answers **three essential questions:**

  1) **WHERE/ WHEN**--Where do I want to go? When do I expect to arrive?

  2) **HOW** am I going to get there?

  3) **WHAT** do I need to do first/ next?

MY GOALS FOR SIX AREAS OF MY LIFE

1. FAMILY

_____

_____

_____

2. FINANCIAL

_____

_____

_____

3. PHYSICAL

_____

_____

_____

4. INTELLECTUAL

_____

_____

_____

5. SOCIAL

_____

_____

_____

6. SPIRITUAL

_____

_____

_____

WHAT TO DO NEXT?

1. Decide the area(s) you can best use your time for the next three months.

_____

_____

_____

_____

2. Implement your immediate goal (WHAT do I need to do first?) until your long-term goal is accomplished. Discuss how.

_____

_____

_____

_____

_____

3. Once you have reached your goal in any area, you then need to set a new goal in that area of your life.

_____

_____

_____

_____

_____

NOW THAT I HAVE ESTABLISHED THE NEED FOR IMPROVED TIME MANAGEMENT, WHAT DO I DO FIRST?

The first step toward improved time management is to analyze how you are currently using your time. In the space provided, record all your activities during the waking hours of one day this week. Divide your day into three segments: (1. wake-up to noon; 2. Noon to 6:00 PM; 3. 6:00 PM to bedtime) and record your activities at the end of each segment (Noon, 6:00 PM, and bedtime).

At the end of the day go through this list of activities, and in the context of the day just completed, attach an A, B, or C priority to each activity using the column on the far right (A=Imperative, it must get done; B=Important, but not urgent; C=Not important, it would be nice to get it done, but...).

Based on your own set of values and your own goals, you are ultimately the only one who can judge the proper priority for each activity. Reminding yourself of your goals may help you but simply because the activity does not appear to place you closer to your goals doesn't mean it is unimportant. Sleeping and eating are examples of activities that are 'A' priorities, when done at the right time.

TIME AWARENESS JOURNAL

SEGMENT NO. 1 (WAKE-UP TO NOON)

TIME	ACTIVITY	A, B, OR C PRIORITY?

SEGMENT NO. 2 (NOON TO 6:00 PM)

TIME	ACTIVITY	A, B, OR C PRIORITY?

SEGMENT NO. 3 (6:00 PM TO BEDTIME)

TIME	ACTIVITY	A, B, OR C PRIORITY?

YOU HAVE COMPLETED THIS ASSIGNMENT, ANSWER THE FOLLOWING QUESTION ABOUT YOUR TIME USAGE:

1.   How many hours did you spend doing 'A' activities?_____

2.   How many hours did you spend doing 'B' activities?_____

3.   How many hours did you spend doing 'C' activities?_____

4. List the kinds of low priority ('C') activities you typically engaged in rather than completing 'A's and 'B's. Which segment of your day do you feel needs the most improvement?

_____

_____

_____

_____

THE NEXT STEP: USING YOUR TIME MORE EFFICIENTLY

You have now clarified how you wish to spend your time in the near future by setting goals in six separate areas of your life. You have also analyzed how you are currently using your time. Chances are, if you are like most people, the reality of how you are spending your time and how you want to spend your time in order to reach your goals are somewhat different.

The following **action exercise** will provide you with a technique you can use daily to help you close the gap between the way it is and the way you want it to be.

HOW TO SET DAILY PRIORITIES TO HELP YOU ACCOMPLISH MORE GOAL-ORIENTED ACTIVITIES.

Time control starts with planning. Planning brings the future into the present so that we can do something about it now. We need to make time choices that are right for our current rather than our past situation. It is important to make a concrete task out of planning. This time can be called 'decision time' because that's what planning is all about making decisions as to WHAT and WHEN.

USING A 'TO DO' LIST TO EFFECTIVELY PLAN YOUR DAY

The purpose of this assignment is to help you plan a day in your life by making a **"TO DO"** list of the specific activities you need to accomplish. By better ordering your day you will relieve much of your distress and be better able to set into action your new eating habit strategies. Here are some directions to help you get the most from this important technique.

1. Make this list before going to bed or first thing in the morning, choosing a day when you anticipate being very busy doing a number of varied tasks.

2. Attach an A, B, or C priority to each activity you list.

    A = Imperative, it must get done
    B = Important, but not urgent
    C = It would be nice to get it done, but...

3. Attach a sequence or order (1, 2, 3...) in which you will do each 'A', 'B', 'C' priority for this day. Each activity will then have a number and a letter (example: A-1, A-2, etc.)

4. Generally, the A's (Imperatives) should be done first. Don't get bogged down in C activities during your prime action time.

5. Ask yourself throughout the day, "What is the best use of my time right now?"

6. Priorities can change quickly. Do not feel badly if you need to add, subtract, or revise as you go through your day.

B   Below is an example of how you can construct your "TO DO" list. For convenience it is best to use a 4 inch by 6 inch piece of paper (or index card).

Although you do not need to include eating situations on your "TO DO" list, keep in mind that eating is an A-1 priority whenever you are hungry. In other words, when you are hungry, eating appropriately is always the best use of your time at that moment.

"TO DO" LIST

SEQUENCE   PRIORITY   ACTIVITY

_____

_____

_____

_____

_____

_____

_____

_____

_____

_____

_____

_____

_____

_____

_____

_____

_____

_____

_____

_____

_____

_____

_____

_____

_____

6

SELF MANAGEMENT PART TWO: WELLNESS AND STRESS

INTRODUCTION: HEALTH AND WELLNESS FOR EFFECTIVE PERFORMANCE

The most common, traditional definition of "health" is the dictionary definition: "free from sickness." Many still harbor the limited belief that if we are not sick, then we must be well or healthy. In addition, personal health care is defined through visits to the doctor. At work we often find employee benefits that reward sickness and disease. This system is more accurately called a "disease care" system, rather than a "health care" system.

Americans can no longer personally or socially afford to be reactive or passive consumers of health, expecting that specialized professionals will repair any damage, regardless of cos that results from lifestyle excesses, poorly planned work structures, and polluted environments. For a number of reasons, many of them related to our need for more efficient use of capital and human resources, the traditional disease model of health care is changing.

American health consumers are learning how to take a more proactive role in the development of improved personal health and employee wellness. The benefits of such a change in strategy are great for improving the productivity and effectiveness of individuals and organizations..

WELLNESS DEFINED

Today, many knowledgeable individuals are looking for something more than the maintenance of their health status-quo. They are seeking something we might call wellness, intrinsic health or positive well-being. In this view, health comes first, while sickness is only the result of the breakdown of this natural and inherent state of positive functioning. This idea of natural or intrinsic wellness focuses upon the whole system, with body and mind, individual and organization synchronized in a state of positive potential and outlook. Wellness includes a zest for living life to its fullest.

Actually the concept was first proposed by Halbert Dunn, Chief of the National Office of Vital Statistics, in the 1950's. Dunn's idea of optimum wellness was based upon the World Health Organization's definition of health (Dunn,1961). Dunn maintained that traditional health was a passive state of homeostasis or equilibrium, while the "process" of wellness was a more dynamic condition of movement toward our optimal health potential.

Dunn's very progressive, yet once controversial, argument based the definition of wellness upon three key areas:

1) Direction of progress;
2) The total individual; and
3) How the individual functions.

This first idea, that movement is toward a goal of higher or optimal functioning, implies that wellness is an active and self-directed process of progress and improvement. Next, is the development of a model of the well-functioning, total person. Finally, is the idea of optimal functioning, total person who is trying to cope with a world of change. Over the years many models of wellness have been built upon this framework.

This view is such a major reversal from the traditional model of health that we must see it as an attempt to change the culture that promotes a narrow, professional control over our health. We must learn to assume more responsibility for this important area of our personal and social well-being.

Wellness is related to the opportunity to maximize one's potential and enlarge one's possibilities for self-knowledge, spiritual growth, emotional harmony, physical contentment and intellectual/mental fitness. It is rooted in our basic biology, yet is much more than that.

Wellness is more than coping, although the ability to be flexible and adaptable is one essential element. It is based upon the important assumption that aging, of itself, does not produce inevitable decline in one's ability to enjoy life to the fullest extent possible.

Wellness is a goal- directed process that recognizes the importance of developing a positive attitude for living. This passion for active living and learning includes the commitment to tasks, projects, and purposes beyond narrow concerns of pure self-interest. These ideas support a quest for multiple, change sensitive, empowering possibilities and not just a search for fads.

LIFESTYLES AND WORKSTYLES

Lifestyle is the typical way we live today. They combine our health and behavioral habits that we have learned over a lifetime, regardless of our current age. In fact, our lifestyle will help determine how long and how enjoyable our life will become in latter years. The very idea of lifestyle indicates that we do have some choice and control over the quality of our lives.

Today, changes in the very foundation of our organizations and institutions present us with an enormous variety of workstyle choices and options. We might define workstyles as the work patterns, habits and behaviors thas make up ourwork personalities. In our highly technological, mobile and information-rich society, we are quite ignorant of our potential and limits. In many ways, the opportunities for active, life-long learning are greater today than ever before.

Since our definition of wellness indicates an active process of taking personal control of your worklife and personal well-being, it should not be confused with current conditions, personal or organizational.

For this reason, awareness through education and assessment is a first important step.

WELLNESS AND CHANGE

We live in an age of rapid change increasing international competition, new trends and fads, and an epidemic of mergers, cutbacks and takeovers. We might call this time the *era of the three C's: accelerating Change, increasing Complexity, and intensifying Competition.* This is also a time of discontinuity, turbulence, and unpredictable events which create great challenges for managers and promoters of wellness. Yesterday's thinking, values and skill development have become increasingly obsolete in a world where constant transformation is the standard, not the exception. Such a situation requires our most creative thinking about wellness.

Dunn believed that the promotion of wellness was quite possible in a world of rapid-paced changes. In fact, it would be even more necessary to face up to reality, learn to ask the right questions, and examine our beliefs and practices about many areas of our lives. Mastering such assessment and life-style change skills is part of our active learning strategy, which Dunn calls adaptation and which I will call learning responsiveness. This response to change can occur at many levels.

One set of strategies for those concerned with the promotion of individual and organizational wellness is learning how to assess, plan, manage, evaluate and promote programs healthy change in: bad personal habits; unhealthy interpersonal relationships; poorly managed work relations and structures; ineffective personal and organizational performance; destructive organizational and personal stress/conflict; and optimal performance for our institutions and organizations (Peters and Waterman,1985).

Accordingly, wellness and health promotion are not concepts with meaning just for individuals and organizations. The relevance of health promotion is in its application to group, family, community and world systems. In fact, it is much easier to ensure personal health when we are supported by well-functioning, optimally healthy systems at many other social levels. We also need to clearly understand the impact these other systems have upon our health and adaptive capabilities. And, of course, optimally functioning people desire and actively support the highest wellness potentials and quality of life for friends, family, and colleagues.

Wellness as we've already stated is a process of constantly moving toward positive and truly optimal performance on a number of interrelated dimensions, whether, intellectual, emotional, spiritual, economic, moral, and social. Whatever dimensions we are concerned with at the time: vision, mission, planning, implementation or evaluation, the key task is anticipating the positive possibilities and staying ahead of the destructive effects of negative thinking and one-dimensional answers. We must also not fear the possibilities inherent in the change process.

Organizational health promotion is a strategic effort by the to reduce the health risks of employees through planned changes in individual risk related behaviors and other organizationally related predisposing conditions. It thus focuses upon changes in both individuals and organizations that reduce risks and thus also tries to enhance the general level of both individual and organizational health, positive functioning and well-being.

This proactive and preventive approach provides the motivational supports and conditions for individuals to examine their behaviors and to decide what needs to be changed and how to change it. These factors can have a profound effect upon any worker's self-esteem and can influence whether they choose to actively participate and support change, productivity and improvement efforts of any type in the workplace

It is believed the group nature of the modern workplace can help individuals to become more motivated to make effective decisions to change their poor health and work habits and for the organization to understand its impacts (through employment practices, managerial behavior and organizational policies) upon the worker. Thus, health promotion, like good human resource development programs, must focus upon approaches that stimulate, motivate and inspire workers and organizations to see the short and long-term impacts of their involvement and contributions.

One of the important ideas to understand when trying to promote good health, productivity, or wellness is that of prevention. What are we trying to prevent? Those poor personal health habits and health practices which lead to negative symptoms in the short-run and to ill health in the long-term. The goal of prevention is to take steps to combat risk factors before a major problem arises. Let's now define some key terms:

Primary change prevention means: using positive early interventions to enable individuals or organizations to avoid the kinds of trouble and problems that might otherwise become very damaging in the long-run. It is based on the idea that the entire population should benefit, and the goal is to promote productive growth and positive strengths rather than to react, heal or restore after positive functioning is no longer possible.

Primary prevention has been generally ignored because it is quite difficult to accomplish. One of the most common techniques is teaching people to alter risky habits and ineffective behavior. A stress reduction program is a good example. Another even more effective, yet more difficult approach is to help people avoid developing bad work habits in the first place.

Secondary change prevention means: that one responds to a situation that has created some problems which have not yet reached crisis dimensions, but it is too late for primary prevention. By catching trouble as early as possible, problems can be addressed before they become a full-blown crisis. The idea is to lessen the impact and extent of the problem. We see the importance of early identification and treatment, such as in a nutrition and health program for those in the early stages of high-blood pressure.

Tertiary change prevention means: that the situation has already deteriorated substantially and the problems are becoming serious. Here, techniques are designed to reduce the consequences of severe dysfunction after its occurrence. These interventions are the most difficult to make effective.

HEALTH BEHAVIORS, HEALTH HABITS AND RISK

Health behaviors are those positive actions that promote health and wellness. Reducing health risks must be part of a more systematic and positive attempt to change health behavior. Health habits are behaviors that are habitual and well established, ones that are performed automatically,   below the level of our conscious awareness.

We develop bad health habits because our initial unhealthy behaviors have been reinforced by positive outcomes or rewards . . Latter, the habit is maintained by social or environmental factors that we associate with that behavior The new. behavior then becomes independent of such rewards Just turn on the TV and watch us run to the kitchen for a snack of extra calories and unhealthy foods like ice-cream, soda and snacks. These habits are very resistant to change. Hence, it is important to establish good behaviors of all types early in life to prevent bad habits from developing.

WHAT INFLUENCES OUR HEALTH BEHAVIOR AND HABITS

Each of us makes daily decisions that directly and indirectly influence our health. The context of these many decisions is varied and complex and includes such influences as friends, media, church, family, clubs, school and business practices. Most of us follow inconsistent patterns of health practices, rules, and habits. Most of the time these practices are influenced by our perceived symptoms, social factors, (like what our family and friends do), our feelings, and access to medical care.

The specific behaviors that make up our lifestyle also impact health and work performance, mostly over the long-term. Over the short-term, poor health habits create vague feelings of being tired, run-down, and irritable. Such symptoms are often viewed as part of the inevitable effects of stress or aging. It is difficult to see that bad health practices lead to serious diseases, like heart attacks, strokes or cancer. These diseases create various costs for individuals and organizations and divert resources away from achieving the organizational vision.

Yes, bad habits and behaviors do determine our wellness and personal effectiveness. Some of these habits are influenced by how we perceive them. For example, if we feel that too many hangovers are keeping us from getting to work on time, we may stop drinking on certain nights of the week or drink earlier in the evening and with dinner to lessen the effects. Perception of negative and bothersome symptoms is often not enough motivation to change poor health habits. We need a more comprehensive approach.

Our culture and society also influences how we view health and why we develop and continue to practice bad habits. We live in a culture that often encourages lost work productivity due to excessive eating, drinking, and smoking, while promoting sedentary and stress-filled lifestyles. Our social/cultural norms encourage poor nutrition habits because of a fast food industry modeled after our fast-paced lifestyle.

Another set of social influences that impact our life, work and health habits are related to those norms, beliefs and values that we learned as children and adolescents. Our parents instilled in us certain habits. These included such practices as how much and what we ate or drank, whether we took vitamins and discussed health as a family issue, and how we learned to value things, including trust, honesty and work.

Finally, friends and peers are social influences that channel our health behaviors by pressuring us into drinking, taking drugs, or using alcohol. Peers have a particularly negative influence upon the smoking and drug taking behavior of adolescents. Peers and colleagues can also have a very positive impact upon our ability to change anything we don't like.

Emotional influences also impact our health behaviors. People often drink, eat and smoke excessively when under high amounts of stress. Remember, a certain amount of stress is essential for active and productive living. A more positive practice to try when under emotional stress is to substitute exercise for excessive eating or drugs. Stress itself can increase under conditions of loneliness and lack of social supports and networks. Mangers need to become more aware of these issues.

MANAGING STRESS AND WELLNESS

Because stress is something that we cannot see or easily measure, and can only feel when we are sensitive to it, we are often unaware of its impact upon us. Individuals and organizations are experiencing many pressures and stresses brought about by numerous social, lifestyle, and technological changes. These changes pose both potential problems and opportunities for learning about how to better manage our personal health, lifestyle, and work relations. Change is a part of life. Without it life becomes monotonous. Challenge and the ability to assert some control over our destiny needs to become part of our motivation to excel.

Stress can be managed; you can make it work for you rather than against you. The mishandling of stress can create all sorts of health, family and work problems in the long-run. In addition, we need to establish more proactive life management skills and wellness strategies.

This section will focus upon several aspects of stress, including: assessment (evaluating, assessing, taking stock of your life); interventions (learning methods, practices, techniques and new habits/skills); and actually implementing change strategies for managing stress and its consequences.

In order to successfully complete any of these aspects of personal stress management, we must begin with our understanding of the various conceptual dimensions of stress. The modern leader, manager, consultant or professional must understand more than how to do something; they must understand why it is done, and when it is appropriate to do one thing rather than another. Once again we see the importance of a systems viewpoint and how actions or sequences of actions in one part of a system impacts other parts of the system..

WHAT IS STRESS?

Hans Seyle (1974, 1976) defined stress as the body's nonspecific reaction/response to any demand placed upon it, whether pleasant or unpleasant. Seyle believed that since stress was the body's nonspecific response, then stress itself can't become responsible for negative outcomes. In fact, some people are able to thrive on stress. The explanatory key for Seyle was the adapted limits of the human body because each of us must become more aware of themselves and not misjudge their capacities by pushing themselves beyond their limits.

Girando and Everly (1969:3) give us a usable but more scientific definition of stress as a *"fairly predictable arousal of the psychophysiological (mind-body) systems which, if prolonged, can fatigue or damage the system to the point of of malfunction and disease."* Stress is really a combination of stressors or factors that elicit a stress response.

WHAT ARE THE THREE BASIC SOURCES OF STRESS?

The three general sources of stress (or stressors) are: **1)** Your personal environment; adjustments must be made constantly to such varied things as noise, weather conditions, time constraints, and threats to your well-being; **2)** Your body; stress is encountered when you are sick, when your nutrition is inadequate, when injuries occur, and when irregularities occur in sleep. Children and adolescents experience stress simply by growing; **3)** Your thoughts/mind; you interpret everyday events your life, and dwell on the bad experiences of the past all cause stress. This is the one source over which you can exert the greatest control by making changes in the way you think. We will discuss specific ways you can work to eliminate these stressors later in this module.

THE NEED FOR STRESS

A minimal or reasonable amount of tension, stress and worry are actually necessary for a healthy life. In fact, it provide the challenge to get us focused and motivated With the belief in our ability to master some life/work skills, we can expand our potential for success, even with temporary defeats.

Stress can help us to clarify and focus upon important life and work goals. So try not to avoid all stress: you can not anyway. In fact, good stress (**eustress**) is essential for motivating high performance. The key is to try to develop a productive perspective about your life priorities, the ratio and amount/type of positive and destructive stress in your life, and your stress response patterns (what is causing you the most stress).

When we observe problems with our responses to stress, we must develop plans to change them. Bad or excessive stress (distress) results from stressors that constantly wear our bodies and minds down by overwhelming our positive problem solving strategies.

WHAT IS THE PHYSIOLOGICAL REACTION TO STRESS?

The release of adrenalin into our blood stream is known as the **General Adaptation Syndrome (GAS), or The Stress Response**. Our body is instinctively ready to "fight" or "flee". We don't need to spend much time reviewing the meaning of these ideas. But the physical impacts of either response on the body can be substantial.

Although these physical responses vary in strength, length and impacts, they follow a fairly simple pattern. The activator stressor(s) signals the hypothalamus in the midbrain (it is not clear whether the signal comes from the frontal cortext or elsewhere). This process activates the pituitary or master gland in the adrenal cortex and the autonamic nervous system (including adrenal glands at the top of the kidneys), and stimulates the production of increased amounts of catechamines, adrenaline and noradrenaline. These stress hormones can ravage even the healthiest body if exposure is prolonged.

STRESS AND THE MIND-BODY LINK

Stress is a product of our mind-body link. It often begins in the mind as an interpretation of the world. Our perceptions of opportunity and risk can lead us to a cycle of either positive or negative behavior. This cycle or system is only effectively changed by feedback Everything we do has a learning lesson attached, if we are receptive and ready for feedback. Failure is only hurtful if we draw too narrow boundaries and miss the learning opportunity.

Without feedback we might suffer from boredom, lack of challenge and social isolation. When people need energy and the will to live, they often force themselves to try new jobs, projects, meet new people, or try some new challenges. People create pain for us., but they also provide our greatest joy and adventures.

Life is truly a constant process of managing work and human relationships. . Those who are good at deciding how to define and solve important problems, experience a type of euphoric stress from the challenge of making headway. Others, with no skills for seeking good information, sharing resources or supports, and joining in on team efforts, are overwhelmed by the sometimes lonely demands of daily life.

The skills we learn and use determine our stress levels. Do we attack problems impulsively and end up feeling defeated and more insecure? Or do we take charge of our lives by learning the skills necessary to decide, organize, interpret and implement a successful, problem-solving process or plan for action.

To prevent feelings of failure and low self-esteem, we must learn good stress assessment and intervention skills and use them during times of uncertainty and frustration. Our inability to organize information into meaningful solutions, creates low self-esteem, which then leads to poor performance and ineffective organizations.

Excessive stress and increased tension can even result from the process of negative thinking itself. Tension levels increase as the images of failure become vivid in our mind. This is why it is important to visualize successful behaviors and understandthat the process of negative cognitive appraisal is as detrimental to our well-being today as the tiger in the jungle was to the well-being our ancestors.

The mind that becomes fixated or preoccupied with sensations of uncertainty and fear of failure, soon creates stress overload, which prevents any open-minded exploration of alternatives. Left unattended, stress incubates, feeds on itself and actually attacks the body with long-term destructive consequences. In fact, scientists are today more comfortable with the term psychophysiological (impacts the body as well as the mind with disease) rather than psychosomatic, which denotes "its all in the mind."

Tension and worry actually get locked into our body and mind, and detract from good decisions. We must utilize our minds to productively visualize problem situations and their solutions. This mental imagery allows us to scan for relevant information and rehearse productive solutions to problems. We need to be free of excessive worry and fear of failure, in order to engage in trial-and-error learning, and use fantasy to positively project future success.

STRESS RESEARCH: SOCIAL READJUSTMENT RATING SCALE

Research by Holmes and Rahe (Gutknecht, et. al., 1988) led to the development of the Social Readjustment Rating Scale (SRRS), which measures the susceptibility to illnesses brought about by various possible life-style of changes. The scale listed 43 specific life events occurring within the last twelve months, each carrying a unit weight (called Life Change Units or LCU'S. The most stressful event was death of a spouse (100 LCU'S), and the lowest was a minor violation of the law (11 LCU'S).

This research shows how broad generic life changes might have impacts upon our vulnerability to illness. However, it does not establish either a cause-effect relationship or the actual incidence of disease. In addition, this model overemphasizes major crises and changes in life events, rather than the cumulative tensions of minor daily hassles and problems can have upon our self-worth and ultimate stress levels. Without the proper perspective, problem solving and diagnostic skills, these bruises to our self-esteem can cause stress overload.

THE RESPONSES TO STRESS

Stressors vary in intensity or strength. They include a wide variety of physical, mental and social-psychological conditions, like too much noise or pollution, changing jobs or even taking on more responsibilities at work. Every change in our lives, whether good or bad, produces a stress response.

When stressors begin to overload our adaptive abilities the following signs or signals result: People under stress often look, feel, and act agitated, nervous, fidgety and can not concentrate or think clearly. They look and feel depleted, passive, drained and depressed. Many individuals suffer from a lack of motivation and may grind their teeth without realizing what they are doing. When under pressure they are hostile, angry and appear out of control. Most can sense that they feel different and something is out of control in their lives.

We each have a unique way of perceiving the world and responding to stress. Our tolerance and ability to control the negative effects of stress results from our ability to recognize stress signals. Without this self-awareness, we experience stress overload.stress. We must learn how to become more aware how to better respond to negative stressors before they create problems. We can learn this skill by assessing and observing our unique stress signals and reactions to stressors. The hardest task for those trying to manage stress is to improve their stress identification skills.

Adams(1978:166-168) has identified four major categories of stres-sors:

1. The changes at work: including job changes such as increased work hours, increased responsibilities, more travel, reorganizations, mergers, changes of work pace and activity level.

2. The nonwork related, major life changes: including taking on an expensive mortgage, other family finances, increased drug use, pregnancy, sexual difficulties.

3. The daily pressures on the job: including limited feed-back, poor communication with your boss, unclear job assignments or responsibilities, excessive work and many tight deadlines.

4. The external environment: that make life tougher, like noise, air pollution, increased traffic and congestion, general concern over the economy, empathy with increased numbers of children who are vistimized by unconcerned adults, etc.

We can identify five main types of reactions to stressors:

1.Subjective: anxiety and low self-esteem
2.Behavioral: accident proneness, excessive eating, and impulsive behavior.
3.Cognitive: the inability to concentrate, forgetfulness, and hypersensitivity to criticism.
4.Physical: high blood pressure, increased glucose levels, dizziness and ulcers.
5.Organizational: increased absenteeism, lower productivity, high turnover, and higher incidence of work related health, accident, or disability claims.

HOW DO "LITTLE HASSLES" LEAD TO BIG PROBLEMS?

For the vast majority of employees, the most immediate source of stress or "stressors" are the "little hassles" which disturb the working day. Most workers can more than adequately fulfill their job description.   Competence is seldom the issue.   Studies and self-reports from working people indicate that it is the minor hassles with other workers, time pressures, or difficult colleagues which constitute the major source of stress in the workplace, especially for office workers.

Prior even to these office or work hassles, small troubles at home can carry over and create stress at work. It is evident that hassles which plague people every day may be more injurious to mental and physical health than major, traumatic life events.

Hassles	Uplifts
1. Concern about weight.	1. Relating well--loved ones
2. Health of a family member.	2. Relating well with friends.
3. Rising prices.	3. Completing a task.
4. Home maintenance.	4. Feeling healthy.
5. Too many things to do.	5. Getting enough sleep.
6. Misplace or losing things.	6. Eating out.
7. Yard work or outside home maintenance.	7. Meeting responsibilities.
8 Investment, or taxes.	8. Visiting or phoning.
9. Crime.	9. Spending time with family.
10. Physical appearance.	10. Home pleasing to you.

None of these may be on your list, but chances are good the small hassles contribute more to your stress than major events.

HOW IS STRESS RELATED TO JOB PERFORMANCE?

It is now a certainty that improved job performance is linked to increased stress up to a certain point but that a point of diminishing return is soon reached.   Excess stress causes performance to deteriorate, whether the task is balancing a checkbook or determining a corporate fiscal policy. This upside-down U-shaped, curvilinear relationship between stress and performance is known as the "Yerkes-Dodson Law."   At the center of the curve is the "performance zone" where manageable stress results in high efficiency and productivity. Too little stress, at the bottom end of the curve, or too much stress, at the top end, cause performance and efficiency to decrease.

Among the many implications of this simple law or principle is that each person has a unique "performance zone" which further varies from day to day. When individuals are within their optimum performance zone, stress results in feelings of energy, excitement, and stimulation, and decisions are readily made. When conditions of stress are underloaded or overloaded, the stress indicators are quite similar, resulting in irritability, a sense of time pressure, diminished motivation, as well as poor judgment and accidents. Fortunately, it is possible for each person to become aware of these facts and develop his or her own unique manner of achieving and remaining within the performance zone. This is one of our primary goals for each participant in this session.

WHICH OF THE FOLLOWING SITUATIONS CAUSE YOU DISCOMFORT AND MAKE YOU FEEL ANXIOUS OR "STRESSED"?

Several prominent researchers have identified the following stressors as most common to management personnel. Check the ones that may apply to you at this point in your career.

[ ]   Work overload and excessive time demands and "rush" deadlines.

[ ]   Erratic work schedules and take-home work.

[ ]   Ambiguity regarding work tasks, territory, and role.

[ ]   Constant change and daily variability.

[ ]   Role conflict (e.g., with immediate supervisor.

[ ]   Job instability and fear of unemployment.

[ ]   Responsibility, especially for people.

[ ]   Negative competition (e.g., "cutthroat, "one-upmanship,"and "hidden aggression."

[ ]   Type of vigilance required in work assignment and "team-building"toward goals.

[ ]   Ongoing contact with "stress carriers" (e.g., workaholics, pas sive- aggressive subordinates, anxious individuals.

[ ]   Sexual harassment.

[ ]   Accelerated recognition for achievement (e.g., Peter Principle).

[ ]   Detrimental environmental conditions of lighting,ventilation\noise, and personal privacy.

It is possible you checked none of the above and yet still experience destructive stress. It is also possible that your body is reacting and producing a stress response to some of the above and you are not aware of it. With virtually all sources of stress, occupational sources included, the first step to better stress management is the simple recognition and clear definition of the source and the type of stressor.

WHAT ARE THE MOST COMMONLY REPORTED WORKPLACE PROBLEMS ASSOCIATED WITH DESTRUCTIVE STRESS?

Studies (Gutknecht, et. al.,1988) indicate that physical impairments resulting from stress in the workplace are as listed below in decreasing order of frequency:

1)   Anxiety and/or Neurosis (25% of reported stress cases).

2)   Depression (20%).

3)   Stress-related, Psychosomatic Disorders (15%)--(Headaches, low back pain, hypertension, gastrointestinal tract).

4)   Alcohol and Drug Abuse (15%).

5)   Situational Adjustment Problems (10%)--(divorce, finances, death in the family).

6)   Other Disorders (15%)--(severe mental and/or physical morbidity or mortality).

From the employer's viewpoint, these impairments show up in the statistics for absenteeism, reduced productivity, and disruption in the workplace.

WHAT ARE THREE POSITIVE STEPS I CAN TAKE TO MANAGE THE STRESS IN MY LIFE MORE EFFECTIVELY?

While stress is not the only thing that causes the physical problems mentioned earlier, their occurrence would be diminished if we:

1) Were better aware of when the stress response was happening,
2) Could reduce the frequency of stress responses, and
3) Had constructive ways of handling them when they occur.

STRESS AWARENESS ASSIGNMENT

The purpose of this exercise is to help you pinpoint the times and events in your day that produce stress, identify the physical symptoms you experience after the stress reaction, and recognize your present way of handling them. Once you have identified these aspects of your stress you will be in a good position to take positive, corrective action.

As you go through your day fill in the categories below. Additionally, for the next week, as you become aware of your stress, refer to this exercise.

STRESS MANAGEMENT MASTER LIST

DATE/TIME	STRESSOR	SYMPTOM FELT	YOUR REACTION

WHAT ARE THE THREE MOST COMMON DESTRUCTIVE STRESS REACTIONS IN THE WORKPLACE?

Individual response to occupational stress can fall into three basic styles: **1)** workaholic behavior; **2)** Type A behavior; and **3)** burnout. Understanding the symptoms related to these is an important first preventive step.

1. Workaholic Behavior

Workaholic is a loosely-defined term which connotes an individual who is addicted to workitsellf, rather than the results of that work. Although the term is usually used in a negative sense, workaholics are not inherently detrimental to themselves or others. A relatively neutral definition has been proposed by Marilyn Machlowitz in **Workaholics: Living With Them, Working With Them** as *"people whose desire to work long and hard is intrinsic and whose work habits always exceed the prescriptions of the job and the expectations of those with whom or for whom they work."* She concluded from her research that *"satisfaction with work and with life are more apt to be intertwined than mutually exclusive."*

This finding is consistent with research in longevity in which job satisfaction has been determined to be a significant predictor of both health and longevity. At the negative extreme there are the impaired workaholics who are inflexibly addicted to work to the detriment of all other dimensions of their lives. Estimates are that approximately 5% of the working population are workaholics.

Workaholic Scale

Check the statements below with which you agree.

[ ] 1. My work is one of the most rewarding and fulfilling parts of my life.

[ ] 2. I would probably work just as much as I do now even if I had no need to work to support myself.

[ ] 3.   One of my main goals in life is to find and do the "work that is play."

[ ] 4.   I use a daily priority list of "things to do" to help me make the best use of my time.

[ ] 5.   Most of my friends would probably agree that I usually have a great deal of energy-and I get much of this energy from my work.

[ ] 6.   I frequently work on weekends and holidays.

[ ] 7.   I am so involved in my work that it is difficult for me to take vacations.

[ ] 8.   I frequently break dates and cancel appointments so that I can get more work done.

[ ] 9.   My work is so much a part of my life that distinctions between "work time" and "time off" get blurred.

[ ] 10.   My involvement in my work sometimes causes problems for my family and friends.

Extreme workaholic tendencies (eight or more) need to be balanced. Here are some suggests for doing this: **1)** focus on the aspects of your work that are most enjoyable and learn to delegate or minimize those that you dislike; **2)** decide how much time you want to spend working and limit your work accordingly; **3)** schedule open time into your work life, since breaks can actually enhance your performance when you return to work; **4)** learn to say "no" to new demands on your time; **5)** try to remain oriented toward the positive aspects of your work such as the freedom and opportunity to be of help to others; **6)** place a value on time away from work; **7)** remember to appreciate your family and friends, since they often feel overlooked and unimportant in the busy blur of a workaholic's productive, but isolated lifestyle.

The good news for workaholics is that high productivity and performance are possible without the disintegration of your personal life, possible heart disease, or psychological burnout. But this situation requires insight and a willingness to initiate small but vital changes in work performance and lifestyle.

2. Type A Behavior

Closely related to the workaholic orientation is **Type A, inflexible, time-pressured behavior**. This has become recognized as a risk factor in heart disease. The following feelings, attitudes, and behaviors are among those that have been used to describe the Type A individual: **1)** easy to anger and has trouble controlling anger; **2)** always in a hurry and feels driven to get things done; **3)** is aggressive and has a strong need for power; **4)** expects perfection from self and others; **5)** impatient and is easily frustrated when things don't work out as expected; and **6)** unreasonably demanding.

The profile below includes many of the characteristics typical of Type A behavior. In the space provided check the characteristics that describe you.

[ ] **1.**   I often think about work when I'm away from my job.
[ ] **2.**   I usually feel guilty when I'm relaxing.
[ ] **3.**   I often interrupt other people when they're speaking.
[ ] **4.**   I can't stand to watch other people doing tasks that I could do faster.
[ ] **5.**   I become irritated when traffic is moving slowly.
[ ] **6.**   I tend to eat my meals quickly.
[ ] **7.**   I always feel rushed.
[ ] **8.**   I enjoy challenging other people's statements and opinions.
[ ] **9.**   I believe that my success is due to my ability to work faster than other people.
[ ] **10.**   I often pretend to listen to other people even though I'm thinking of other things.

If you checked *more than four items*, there is a good chance that you have some *Type A tendencies*. This is not necessarily bad, but it is important for you to be aware of some of the consequences of the stress that can result from Type A behavior.

HOW DIFFICULT IS IT TO CHANGE IF I HAVE SOME TENDENCIES TOWARD TYPE A BEHAVIOR?

Many researchers believe that changing Type A behavior is easier than changing eating habits. Some simple strategies for change, recommended by Carl Thoresen, a Stanford psychologist, include: 1) talking more slowly and less emphatically; 2) interrupting others less and focusing your full attention on what they have to say; 3) gesture less abruptly with your head and hands; 4) cut down on fidgeting and juggling, and 5) find humor in the situation.

Our society seems to reward typical Type A individuals by recognizing their accomplishments, admiring the speed at which they complete tasks, giving them promotions in the organization, electing them to public office. But what price are some of these people paying for their success? We do not ask you to change your personality simply because you may exhibit some of these characteristics. We would only ask that you take a close look at the ways in which your attitudes and behaviors contribute to stress, and then explore ways to modify some of these behaviors to lower your stress load.

3. Burnout

Among the characteristics of burnout are chronic fatigue, low energy, irritability, and a negative attitude toward one's self and one's job. In listening to individuals suffering from burnout, certain themes consistently emerge, such as "trapped or attacked," "need to get away or escape," feeling weighted down," "exhaustion or depletion," "sensation of emptiness and loneliness," "being blocked by obstacles or circumstances which are insurmountable," and finally, "giving up or drowning."

At the workplace these personal feelings translate into difficulty concentrating on or making decisions, failure of short-term memory, and overall impatience, cynicism, irritability, and rigidity or resistance to new input and ideas. Burnout seems to have three phases: **First**, there is emotional exhaustion, a feeling of being drained, used up, and of having nothing more to give. **Second**, there is a cynicism, a callous, insensitive regard for people, a "don't knock yourself out for anyone" attitude. **Finally**, the burnout victim comes to believe that he or she has been unsuccessful and all job effort has been fruitless.

Although burnout affects both men and women at every level of employment, it is not inevitable, and its treatment or prevention can be as simple as one executive's decision to "make sure that every day I sit down with a real person and talk about a real problem, instead of pushing paper around."

As with workaholic or Type A behavior, it is possible to give an assessment of burnout tendencies. Below is a self-administered scale which can indicate such tendencies. *Respond to this quiz by thinking back over the last six months of your life.* Read each question and then give yourself a score for each one, ranging from **"1" indicating "little or no change" in the last six months** in the item, **to "5" indicating a "good deal of change"** in the item. Allow yourself about 30 seconds for a response and add up the total number of points to the 15 items as your final score for a maximum of 75.

THE BROWNOUT/BURNOUT INVENTORY

Please **check** the items that pertain to you.

[ ] **1.**   Do you tire more easily? Feel fatigued rather than energetic?

[ ] **2.**   Are people annoying you by telling you, "You don't look too good lately?"

[ ] **3.**   Are you working harder and harder and accomplishing less and less?

[ ] **4.**   Are you increasingly cynical and disenchanted?

[ ] **5.**   Are you often invaded by a sadness you can't explain?

[ ] **6.**   Are you forgetting appointments, deadlines, possession?

[ ] **7.**   Are you increasingly irritable, short tempered, and/or disappointed in the people around you?

[ ] **8.**   Are you seeing close friends and family members less frequently?

[ ] **9.**   Are you too busy to do even routine things like make phone calls, read reports, or send out Christmas cards?

[ ] **10.**   Are you suffering from physical complaints (aches, pains, colds)?

[ ] **11.**   Do you feel disoriented when the activity of the day comes to   a halt?

[ ] **12.**   Is joy elusive?

[ ] **13.**   Are you unable to laugh at a joke about yourself?

[ ] **14.**   Does sex seem like more trouble than it's worth?

[ ] **15.**   Do you have very little to say to people?

Give yourself 5 points for each item checked. SCORE____

As with the previous workaholic scale and Type A checklist, **do not be alarmed if your score is high (51 to 75).** These self-administered scales are not definitive by any means. Actually, the greatest value of such self-administered scales is to take the first step toward correcting burnout tendencies by recognizing them. Once the recognition occurs, it is then possible to consider alternative choices of action.

WHAT CHARACTERISTICS ARE PRESENT IN THOSE MANAGERS WHO SEEM RESISTANT TO STRESS?

Dr. Suzanne Kobasa of University of Chicago has defined certain qualities in stress resistant people. She studied 259 executives over a two year period. At the end of two years it was evident that the executives who remained healthy under stress had certain characteristics in common which Kobasa termed "hardiness." These executives displayed three characteristics: 1) A sense of commitment to, rather than alienation from the various aspects of their lives; 2) A belief that they have control over their lives rather than feeling externally controlled, and 3) A search for novelty and challenge rather than familiarity and security. Those executives who remained healthy had an attitude toward life and their work which was high on commitment, challenge, and control, and felt supported in that orientation.

TECHNIQUES TO HELP YOU MINIMIZE THE IMPACT OF THE STRESS RESPONSE.

Ultimately, your success in managing stress depends on your ability to find and consistently use one or more stress management techniques. Read each alternative below and decide which one(s) you will be able to initiate for each stressful situation you encounter.

SELF-TALK

This refers to the technique discussed above which explains how you can use your reasoning ability to stop a negative, destructive emotional response to a potential stressor. This should be one of the first options you investigate when confronted by a situation that has previously controlled you. Most of the following alternatives are ways to deal with destructive stress once it has occurred.

THOUGHT STOPPING

This refers to the technique of stopping stressful thoughts as soon as you become aware of them. Follow these simple steps to implement this technique:

1.   Identify your recurring negative thought patterns (e.g., "I hate feeling so stressed all the time." "I'm out of control of my stress.")

2.   Write these thoughts down adding key words that describe a more positive or desirable alternative (e.g., "I'm gaining control of my stress and feeling better every day." "I'm consistently improving and I feel much better about myself.").

3.   When you become aware that you are experiencing negative thoughts about yourself, yell "STOP". Do this mentally if you are in a crowd.

4.   Then, plug in the new statement about yourself to develop a positive mental picture. Work to build this image for at least two minutes. Repeat as often as possible.

DEEP BREATHING TECHNIQUE

This is the one alternative you can easily use every time you encounter stress and can be used in conjunction with every other technique. The major physiological benefit of this is an immediate reduction in your heart rate. Here is the simplest way to use this technique:

1.   Take a deep breath, drawing oxygen deep into your lungs.
2.   Hold this breath for 3 seconds.
3.   Slowly exhale forcing all the air out of your lungs.
4.   Repeat this two additional times.
5.   Wait one minute and repeat this exercise again.

EXERCISE

This can be used as a daily stress reduction technique and is highly effective when done aerobically for 20 minutes at approximately 70% of your maximum heart rate. (Consult your physician before beginning any new exercise regimen.)

SELF-VISUALIZATION

This is another form of self-talk. Here are some self-talk images to practice that will help you see yourself as a calm and centered person who is not controlled by events and the people around you. Feel free to make up your own scripts.

1.   I am calm. Nothing makes me upset. I am composed and in control at all times. Every day in every way I become more serene.

2.   When I start to feel frustrated and angry, I simply identify the source and detach myself from it. I can easily separate myself from the source, and I choose not to identify with it personally.

3.   I have a good sense of humor. I am funny. Laughing makes me feel good and less tense. When I'm frustrated I laugh a lot. I love to smile and laugh.

4.   When my life becomes stressful, I remember my goals. I am patient. I know what I want and I ignore minor setbacks. I feel tranquil and positive when I focus on my goals.

THE RELAXATION RESPONSE

Dr. Herbert Benson has developed a highly effective technique that can reverse the bodily reactions that occur during The Stress Response. He reports that the same center of the brain that speeds up your biochemical processes when you are alarmed can be called upon to slow these processes down.

This process is called the *Relaxation Response*. When this technique is practiced correctly and consistently it will cause your pupils, hearing, blood pressure, heartbeat, respiration, and circulation to return to normal.

Four components necessary to bring about this response are: **1)** A quiet environment; **2)** A mental device (a sound, word, or phrase repeated silently or aloud); **3)** A passive attitude toward your

environment; and **4**) A comfortable position is recommended).
A)
The relaxation technique

1.   Sit quietly in a comfortable position.

2.   Close your eyes.

3.   Deeply relax all your muscles, beginning at your feet and progressing up to your face. Keep them relaxed.

4.   Breathe through your nose. Become aware of your breathing. As you breathe out, say the word, "ONE" silently to yourself. For example, breathe IN...OUT, "ONE"; etc. Breathe easily and naturally.

5.   Continue for 8 to 20 minutes. You may open your eyes to check the time, but do not use an alarm. When you finish, sit quietly for several minutes, at first with your eyes closed and later with eyes opened. Do not stand up for a few minutes.

6.   Do not worry about whether you are successful in achieving a deep level of relaxation. Maintain passive attitude and permit relaxation to occur at its own pace. When distracting thoughts occur, try to ignore them by not dwelling upon them and return to repeating "ONE". With practice, the response will come with little effort. Practice the technique once or twice daily, but not within two hours after any meal, since the digestive process seems to interfere with the elicitation of the Relaxation Response.

TIME MANAGEMENT

Almost all of us could benefit from better use of our productive time during the work day. If you consistently reach a point in the day when you feel frustrated and anxious because of your failure to accomplish what you felt was important, you are experiencing destructive stress. Awareness of the causes of poor time management is the first step to better use of this precious commodity. Below is a series of statements which represent seven of the most common symptoms of poor time management (see chapter 6 for more in-depth coverage of this topic)

8. NUTRITION

Good nutrition can help you insulate yourself from the physical symptoms of stress. Take the following test to help you determine some of the strong and weak points in this area of your life.

MY PERSONAL NUTRITION TEST

Check [/] the items that are true for you *(most)* of the time:
I eat or drink...

[ ] **1.** Less than three eggs per week.

[ ] **2.** No more than two cups of coffee or two cola beverages per day.

[ ] **3.** Whole grain breads, and avoid white bread as much as possible.

[ ] **4.** Four or more servings of grains each day (bread, pasta, rice, etc.).

[ ] **5.** No more than 1 oz. of "hard" alcohol or two beers or glasses of wine per day.

[ ] **6.** No more than one highly concentrated sugar item per day (candy, donut, cake, etc.).

[ ] **7.** Two servings or more of low fat, high protein items per day (lean red meat, light chicken meat, dried peas or beans, or fish).

[ ] **8.** At least two fresh fruits (or juice) per day.

[ ] **9.** At least two servings of vegetables per day.

[ ] **10.** No more than 1/2 teaspoon of added salt each day.

how to interpret your results

1.   If you checked two or less of the above items as true for you, your diet needs some immediate corrective action!

2.   If you scored between three and six your diet is marginal.

3.   If you scored seven or more your diet is probably fairly balanced.

This test is one way you can gauge the progress you make in the area of nutrition. When you have had an opportunity to implement positive changes in your diet, take this test again.

SUMMARY OF THE STEPS TO SUCCESSFUL STRESS MANAGEMENT

STEP #1   Become aware of your own stress and your stressors.

STEP #2   Understand what stress is and the long-term negative effects it can cause.

STEP #3   Become aware of some of your bodily responses to stress.

STEP #4   Pinpoint the times and events in your day that produce stress.

STEP #5   Implement proven techniques to help yourself eliminate as much stress as possible.

STEP #6   Practice one or more positive stress reduction techniques to help yourself minimize the impact of destructive stress.

7

ORGANIZATIONAL HEALTH PROMOTION: ASSESSING, PLANNING, IMPLEMENTING, EVALUATING AND PROMOTING

INTRODUCTION

The discussion of organizational health promotion will help us to perceive the importance of applying the framework developed in earlier chapter to a strategic area of organizational life. We are essentially talking about the process of assessing, planning, implementing, developing, promoting and evaluating programs.

We must learn to perceive human resource issues in more creative ways. To use the language and concepts of investment, we need to invest in the maintenance of our human capital, just as we invest in the maintenance of physical capital. In many organizations when it comes to developing business strategies, the view of people as an important organizational asset however, is only given lip service. Yavitch (1988: 35-40) suggests that there are several reasons for this this paradox of ignoring the corporation's primary asset.

First, in historical perspective, Taylor and other proponents of Scientific Management emphasized human labor as a cost component and not an important determinant of production strategy. A second, more pervasive factor is the treatment of human assets in conventional accounting practices. Employees are designated in the operating statement as an expense, which is even interpreted as a variable (short-term, readily liquidated and easily reacquired) expense. These conventions are not the fault of business, or unions who have-also supported a shot-term outlook; they are merely reflections of past historical experience. In a changing international marketplace, we need to rethink these conventions along the lines of other societies who view employees as a long-term asset and an obligation of doing business.

Finally, the third reason is the basic difficulty of analyzing, measuring and quantifying the many components of human resources:

1) What is the "productive capacity" of a worker?

2) At what point do we reach the limit of a worker's talent or capability? Is this a limit on the volume of work he or she can handle)?

Some researches, like Odiorne (1984) have tried to surmount these difficulties by developing a *portfolio approach* to the categorization of human assets. In the narrow business sense, maybe we can at least begin to think of ways for maintaining our assets, whether capital or human, so they can return their investment over the longest period possible. This strategy will start us thinking about using more rigorous categories to measure performance to show that our people do make a difference to our success.

What is preventive maintenance for physical capital? A system of documentation and ongoing monitored procedures to insure that all equipment is maintained in peak operating condition so as to eliminate costly breakdowns. Ultimately these essential maintenance services allow the organization to build the groundwork for improved productivity.

Emery Air Express is an excellent example of a company with an excellent program of investment for preventive maintenance. Some newer airlines are being called on the carpet for their failure in this regard. Service organizations and consulting firms who practice needs-based marketing are good examples of organizations who understand the importance of proactive strategies for preventive maintenance of all assets, including the clients they serve.

Another issue that makes our task of measuring and recognizing human resources as assets more difficult is the need to make a distinction between machines which break down more readily and people who are capable of refreshing and rejuvenating themselves. Although people are more renewable than machines, they are not infinitely so. People can rebound from failure and retrain themselves for future successful performance. However, once neglect and extensive damage results in long-term degeneration or disease, the process of repair or replacement produces only marginal results for both people and machines.

The failure to care for our assets, whether with physical or human assets, produces both direct and indirect costs to the organization. This is sometime ignored when speaking of human resources because an unhealthy workplace (not concerned with prevention) produces costs that are often submerged into the idea that people are different from and can't be compared with machines. This is the kind of danger that an idealistic viewpoint fails to adequately address. The interesting part of our analogy is that it fits better with a philosophy of the material world.

Let's document some of these direct and indirect costs. Direct costs include salary, medical costs, rehabilitation, survivor benefits, and workman's compensation. The indirect costs include distress and disorganization, pay for temporary workers and overtime for others, training for temporary workers, retraining and rehabilitation for workers who resume work after long absences, costs for turnover, recruitment, selection, hiring replacements and other administrative costs.

The U.S. Chamber of Commerce documents that organizations spent $2560 per worker for health care in 1985, which is up 10% since 1977. This amounts to about 11.8% of the average payroll. Another startling statistic is that companies spent 24% of their total net profit in 1983 on health insurance and .11% (that is right, less than 1 %) on health promotion or prevention. In 1983, health care costs at Chrysler added $600 to the price of every car produced.

And finally, we know that approaches such as human resources and health promotion help individuals and organizations control the costly risk factors associated with disease and associated productivity sapping expenses. Whether we eat, exercise, smoke, drink excessively, fail to communicate or resolve conflict, design jobs poorly or give poor appraisals, they all contribute to a drain upon personal life expectancy, worker morale, turnover, absenteeism, and organizational productivity. The facts are overwhelming for anyone with an open mind and a tough skin; both something human resource people need more than ever before.

People who are 40% overweight, are absent from work twice as much as other workers and add an average $1000 in general health and work-related cost to every employer in this country (this of course varies for organizational size and industrial sector). Obesity dramatically increases the risk of back pain, injury and heath-related costs, including workman's compensation. One estimate is that 93 million workdays and 14 billion dollars are lost to organizations as a result of obesity. Smoking costs organizations $65 billion and costs society over $100 billion annually.

All of these facts lead us to the need for human resource and health promotion programs. Organizational health promotion is a strategic effort to reduce the health and lifestyle risks of employees through planned changes in individual behaviors and other organizationally-related predisposing conditions. Health promotion thus focuses upon changes in both individuals and organizations to reduce risks for both.

The team orientation of the modern workplace can help individuals to become more motivated to make effective decisions to change their poor health and work habits and for the organization to understand its sometimes negative impact (through employment practices, managerial behavior and organizational policies) upon the worker. Thus, health promotion must focus upon new approaches that stimulate, motivate and inspire workers and organizations to see their mutual interests and the productive potential of working together (see chapter 2).

ORGANIZATIONAL HEALTH PROMOTION

Health promotion is the term most often used when discussing the application of health and wellness strategies and principles (including the behavioral changes discussed in chapters 5 and 6) to institutions and organizations. Health promotion can be defined as the systematic efforts by institutions and organization to prevent illness, disease or premature death of its employees through education, behavior change and cultural/organizational supports. Our concern is for the process of good interaction and communication, as well as high-level system development.

The key idea is that everybody and all systems, regardless of current condition, are capable of making significant improvements. Wellness and health promotion, therefore, are not a final landmarks reached and then dropped, but rather a continual process of healthy living and relating that involve numerous components of positive, high-level functioning.

Today, over 50,000 companies offer various health and fitness programs. About half of American companies with 50 or more employees have some sort of wellness program. Most of these have their origin during the 1970's as a result of attempts to deal with executive and managerial stress, heart disease, burnout and other health factors related to costly early retirement, turnover, costs for recruitment or training and the untimely and early deaths of these key personnel. As these programs grew and were extended, it became clear that they could produce gains in productivity, reduce health care claims, and increase worker satisfaction.

A survey of wellness programs by Solomon (Gutknecht, 1988) revealed some interesting results: 1) that the most common type of company with a wellness program was in the consumer goods sector, while the least common was in the manufacturing sector; 2) that 89 percent of the 28 companies who responded to the survey had fairly diverse goals for their programs: including reducing health care costs (16), increasing productivity (13), improving performance (11), enhancing the company's image (9), protecting the employee (9), boosting morale (8), and aiding recruitment (5).

A Gallup Poll indicated that 62% of employees who began exercising found new energy, while 46% felt more confident, 44% experienced greater job satisfaction, and 37% reported increased levels of creativity in the office. An experiment conducted with NASA employees found that 50% of their employees who adhered faithfully to an exercise program reported more positive attitudes toward their jobs (Gutknecht, et. al., 1988).

AN INTEGRATED WELLNESS/HEALTH PROMOTION PROGRAM

The way to increase personal accountability (cost of health utilization organizations) for health is to recognize that both individuals and organizations make decisions that impact them based upon several life issues and many dimensions: spiritual, physical, social, cultural, emotional and intellectual. Good decisions about life-style and work behavior are based upon good information, skills, rewards, and supports, which help us to make important changes in our life-style and organizational behaviors.

We can identify **four levels for organizational health promotion** that correspond to the stages of individual health promotion discussed in chapter 5. Let's briefly review these stages. The **first level** is focused upon awareness and information contained in introductory talks about health promotion or payroll stuffers on changing negative health behaviors.

The **second level** is general health information, along with structured programs, i.e., hypertension control screenings and Health Risk Appraisals (HRA). These serve to determine risk factors or predisposition to disease. This motivational level begins to help the individual to consolidate some of the information gained through awareness and begins to make behavioral change more relevant and likely.

The **third level** is composed of fairly comprehensive health promotion programs that focus upon intervention systems for ongoing behavioral change. These include enlarged opportunities for promoting change through human resource incentives, rewards and supporting policies.

The **fourth level** is concerned with organizational change. It contains programs that address the full range of structural and leadership issues. At this level we can find such topics as organizational work redesign, cultural change, organizational philosophy, values, norms, and management styles

We need to learn how to make our organizational cultures promote positive values, health promotion and life-long personal, organizational and community wellness. We need to find ways to encourage a greater awareness of the trends that are destructively impacting our society, organizations and individual lives. We can only accomplish these tasks by viewing the organization as an interdependent, open-system with structural, policy and behavioral health impacts.

This process requires a comprehensive approach. When employees feel the bad health effects of inconsistent and unclear work policies, poorly designed jobs and rapidly increasing stress levels, we find that disability claims dramatically increase. In such situations, organizations should not assume that simply providing adequate benefits (or adding co-payments) will solve the problems of excessive health care utilization, increased health care costs, absenteeism, and turnover.

These problems are often designed into the organizational culture, policies and structures. So they must be addressed, just like other preventable problems, low productivity and poor work quality, as part of a total organizational approach. In addition, we cannot expect miracles over the short-run. We need to create long-term solutions. Let's become more proactive and not wait until a crisis requires us to react with half-hearted and half-baked efforts and programs.

ORGANIZATIONAL HEALTH PROMOTION : A SMALL BUSINESS CASE STUDY

In 1979, in a small lumber company in Minnesota, a middle-age employee, basically in the prime of life, dropped dead of a heart attack. He was overweight, had hypertension, and exhibited a "driving" personality.

This family business, Scherer Brothers Lumber Company, witnessed the premature death of two other employees around this same time, one from a preventable yard accident and the other from suicide following a forced early retirement due to arteriosclerosis. According to Gregg Scherer, "Three good employees, three lives lost, three deaths which could have been prevented through a program of active intervention. These situations are not isolated, they happen in all corporations. When reduced to simplistic terms we were dealing with factors such as poor nutrition, lack of exercise, inability to control stress, and poor safety habits; all factors which take these tragedies out of the realm of fate and put them squarely in the arena of corporate responsibilities" (Scherer, 1983).

Scherer Brothers decided to do something about these occurrences. Out of this concern, the company conducted a needs assessment to determine employee interests regarding health promotion programs. The company then proceeded to create a low-cost, highly effective health promotion program based upon the following mission: "To create and support a healthy lifestyle and attitude both in the workplace and at home."

Some of the policies included: Removing all candy and cigarette machines from the work environment and replacing them with fruit dispensing ones; eliminating salt from all company food; and substituting decaffeinated coffee in the vending machines. In addition, programs on smoking cessation and nutrition were established. Although not the first small business to develop a comprehensive health promotion effort, it remains to this day one of the most successful, as well as one of the more highly visible.

This story is an excellent model for businesses everywhere. The model is actually quite simple--it is based upon the overwhelming recognition that; health care costs are rising dramatically, poor health practices are creating great tragedy in the ranks of our workers colleagues, and even close friends; and employee morale is suffering.

The premise that guides this chapter and this book as we've already stated is that we must learn to identify and invest in linking personal and organizational issues, like health promotion and organizational productivity. Effectively managed organizations must recognize that the growing health promotion movement is neithera fad nor extravagance. Health promotion is here to stay as an important component of any optimally functioning organizational system. The Insurance industry is one that is taking a particularly strong leader-ship role in this area.

The planning of any personal or organizational effort must begin with an assessment of needs: individuals employees, various groups, and divisions in the organization. No planning effort will be effective unless these are clearly understood and articulated. The results will more accurately reflect the needs and interests of the organization when feedback is obtained.

Key issues and decision points arise during this first assessment or-ganizational activity. Among the questions crucial to moving forward with the effort are the following: Will upper management support the effort to the extent needed? Is the employee-employer relationship conducive to a successful effort? Can the needs expressed during this activity be translated into clearly definable goals? Are the reasons the various entities say they want something, the "right" ones? (For example, if the only reason a CEO wants a new program is to improve productivity and reduce costs in a short span of time, is this realistic?) These are a few of the issue that need some thought before extensive planning begins.

THE IMPORTANCE OF NEEDS ASSESSMENT

Three of the most important reasons to assess input from all management levels in a company are:

1. To help plan an overall effort that has a good chance of succeeding.

2. To enable all the employees to feel a part of the program (a perception of system-wide ownership is important).

3. To sell yourself and the strengths of the program.

SAMPLES OF NEEDS ASSESSMENTS MATERIALS

To obtain the best picture possible of the organizational needs and issues, the project or program planner should interview employees at the following organizational levels, given the organization is large enough to have these positions: the CEO (or upper management spokesperson for the CEO); the Director of Benefits, the Human Resource Manager or Personnel Director; one or more Middle Managers;), and as many line employees as possible.

With the exception of the Preprogram Survey, which is the most generic of the assessments, all surveys are best conducted as one-to-one interviews. When data is needed, such as absenteeism or turnover figures, ask the interviewee how much time he/she needs to obtain the answer, and call back for that date. A personal interview will assure managers of the importance of your project and that the assessment gets completed; self-assessment instruments and surveys usually are viewed as lower priority tasks and completed accordingly.

The Preprogram Survey: This is a general survey that can serve more than one purpose. An outside consultant may wish to use it to screen a company to determine the level of interest in a particular program. Since this instrument is not specifically designed for one-to-one interviewing, much time can be saved. An employee/ coordinator may also derive benefit from using it in this way. Some sample issues covered survey are shown below. For a more complete discussion of this issues and examples of each type of survey discussed above, please see **Designing Health Promotion Systems: Strategies for Individual Wellness and Organizational Health** (Gutknecht, et. .al.:1988).

THE OPEN SYSTEMS APPROACH TO PROGRAM PLANNING

Many workplace health promotion programs fail before they begin, and die in the planning stage. Why programs sometimes miss their mark is an important question to examine if we are to understand their full potential for promoting health in the workplace.

An open systems approach is defined in this context as an analysis of the values, behaviors, and patterns of interactions that impact the effective functioning of all the parts of a given system. Because a system is composed of many constantly changing, interdependent parts, a more comprehensive perspective is often needed to insure the practical application of concise objectives tied to achievable outcomes.

An opens systems approach is needed in the field of health promotion because of the complexity of the human, social, organizational, and program challenges facing those involved. An open systems approach is used to increase the effectiveness of health promotion programs by meeting the following objectives:

THE EIGHT OBJECTIVES OF THIS APPROACH AS APPLIED TO HEALTH PROMOTION PLANNING ARE:

1.   Identify work and health problems areas.
2.   Pinpoint existing problems in the organization that might affect program success.
3.   Increase cost-effectiveness of the program by looking at the "big picture."
4   Provide data useful in program planning and goal setting.
5.   Increase program impact by understanding the organization
6.   Encourage participation and support throughout the organization.

7.   Increase long term benefits and provide follow-up data on emerging problems, trends, and challenges in the organization.
8.   Create data helpful for further planning, manpower, and human resource concerns of the organization.

The **goal of the implementation phase** is to make the transition from the program plan to the successfully operating program. An effectively managed implementation plan is as important to the overall success of the program as an effective program plan. In fact, the implementation phase requires more precise supervision than the design phase. If errors are made during the design phase, they can be corrected by redoing that portion of the design. To correct errors committed during the implementation phase, the damage caused by the errors must be corrected before that portion of the implementation is revised.

FIVE ISSUES CENTRAL TO SUCCESSFUL IMPLEMENTATION

The following five questions can serve as a guide to planning the implementation phase of an organizational health promotion program.

1.) What are the program components that need to be implemented? The answer to this question can be derived from the data gathered during the planning stage. For example, we will say that one of the programs to be implemented is smoking cessation. This will allow us to address the four issues below:

2.)   What are the steps required to implement each component?

A.   Determine the level of need and interest in the program. This is also an issue that is often decided in the planning stage. Employee surveys can help answer the pertinent questions, i.e, do we have enough interest to begin a smoking cessation program?

B.   Examine program options and choose one.
Which stop smoking program will we provide? Will one with a higher success rate and higher costs be more beneficial that one that

is lower in both success rate and cost?

C. Plan program logistics.
Dates, times, manpower, and budget are key issues here. Timing is especially important. The best time to start a smoking cessation is in January. The worst time is in December.

D. Begin marketing effort/introduce program to employee prospects. This step continues until program is implemented. Marketing may include articles in newsletter concerning harmful effects of smoking, and/or announcement of upcoming program. Brochures, flyers, bulletin board announcements, announcements and/or memo from CEO are also considerations. An introductory meeting where employee can meet with program presenters and hear about the program in a non-pressure environment is strongly advised.

E. Implement program.
If the other steps are done correctly, this one should not present last minute surprises and problems.

3.) What are the major timetable for each of the steps mentioned in two? (The following is a timeline one might use for implementation of a smoking cessation program.)

A.   6 MONTHS BEFORE YOUR PLANNED START DATE--Determine the level of need and interest in a stop smoking program.
B.   4 MONTHS BEFORE--Examine program options and choose one.
C.   3 MONTHS BEFORE--Plan program logistics.
D   1 MONTHS BEFORE--Begin marketing efforts and introduce program to employee prospects.
E.   DAY ZERO--Implementation of program begins

4.) What resources, funding, space, technological assistance, and people are required for each step?

This step addresses such issues as:

   A.   Will our program provide incentives and rewards?

    B.   Where will the class be held and at what time of day?
    C.   What support staff will be needed to implement the program?
    D.   What will the marketing effort include?

5.) What are the measures of success? What criteria will we use to determine individual success in this program?   What additional criteria can we use to measure organizational success? For example when a program participant quits smoking and remains quit for a period of one year, he/she will be considered a success for the purpose of measurement. If this success results in a significant reduction in absenteeism and health care claims costs for the group as a whole, the program will be considered successful.

IMPLEMENTATION CHARACTERISTICS OF SUCCESSFUL HP ACTIVITIES

What common features are seen in behavior change programs that achieve successful results? Wellness components come in all shapes and sizes. We will discuss some of their differences in a later segment of this chapter. Not all of the aspects described here are present in successful lifestyle change programs, but many are. Below are listed some aspects we have identified as important.

    1. One-to-one interaction--Although this is not a common feature of workplace wellness programs, many of the best programs-those that have the greatest impact on participants seem to support a high level of personal interaction.   In the case of assessment programs (i.e., Health Risk Appraisals, Fitness Testing, e.g.), this is important for motivational and educational reasons.   In behavior change programs, personal interaction with a health professional or program presenter can provide valuable feedback and at the same time transmit an "I care" feeling.

    2. Group support--Many professionals (e.g., Allen, 1984) feel that group support is necessary for maintenance of major lifestyle changes. Allen goes beyond the normal group interaction, to talk of cultural support. Supportive environments away from the workplace are imperative for maintenance of long-term lifestyle changes. As noted earlier, the built-in support system provided by the work environment is one of the reasons long term success rates are higher for workplace programs.

3. Follow-up by health professionals--For programs where medical compliance is a major issue--diabetes and hypertension, among others--the importance of follow-up is clearly documented. Program components have a clear beginning and an ending. However, in instances where health professionals or HP coordinators take the time to follow-up, the anecdotal evidence seems highly favorable. Consider the employee who is recognized and rewarded at the end of one year for sustaining a major behavior change.

4. Upper management support--Where upper management is involved in a positive way, through participation, recognition, and reward giving, health promotion is usually interpreted as a positive employee benefit.

5. Voluntary participation--Not only is this a characteristic of a successful program, along with confidentiality, it is a necessary condition. With the exception of safety programs that are enacted to meet OSHA requirements (and possibly a few other exceptions), a wellness program relies heavily upon volunteeism . The cornerstone of the wellness movement is personal responsibility and when participation in a wellness promotion program is mandated, a vital ingredient necessary for personal growth is missing.

6. Confidentiality--All manner of problems arise, including legal ones, when this is compromised. Health promotion coordinators need not only take every precaution to ensure that privacy is protected, but they must communicate this to prospective participants. Unless otherwise told, many employees will assume that written records will be available to supervisors or upper managers.

EVALUATION ISSUES

Evaluation of human resource activities of any kind within organizational settings is one of the most important in the whole field of HR. The task of evaluating health promotion activities is even newer and less understood. It recalls the story of the pilot who spoke to his passengers over the airplane intercom system in mid-flight, "Ladies and gentlemen, good afternoon. This is your captain speaking. I have two announcements to make--one good and one bad. First the good one; we are making excellent time! Now the bad news; we are lost!"

We do vast amounts of training, education, and development in human resources including, in recent years, health promotion programs. Yet do we know how effective our programs really are? The issue of accountability relates to a very basic question asked by all responsible organizations: What have you done with the resources we have given you?

Too often, evaluation of programs, products, and services is given only casual attention. Even though the evaluation comes after the planning, assessment, and implementation stages, decisions about what is to be evaluated, who will be doing the evaluation, the manner in which the evaluation is to occur, and, finally, the uses for information obtained in the evaluation process need to be made prior to the assessment and implementation stages.

The measurement and evaluation of program outcomes has become the single most important activity in the still young field of health promotion, according to several prominent researchers (Opatz, 1987). Early organizational supporters of health promotion programs, were personally committed to encouraging wellness programs because they "made sense." But the time for blind acceptance of health promotion efficacy has passed.

Some programs that had foregone evaluation of their programs in favor of investing those dollars in program activities are in deep trouble. Corporate executives are asking for data to support the continuation of long-standing and in some cases, very expensive programs. the data is backing them up. Other organizations that are establishing a new program are setting clear expectations for measurable outcomes.

DEFINING KEY TERMS USED IN EVALUATION

Definition of Evaluation: *"The systematic collection, analysis and interpretation of data for the purpose of determining the value of a social policy or program, to be used in decision-making about the program."* (Moberg, 1984)

There are three key aspects to this definition. **First**, data collection is systematic. It is planned for in advance and follows specific procedures for sampling, documentation, verification, and validation. **Second,** the value or merit of a program must be determined, either relative to other alternative activities, or to a set of goals or criteria of value or success. **Third,** the purpose of evaluation sets it apart from other forms of research by the fact that evaluation is to be used in decision-making about the program.

Too often, evaluation of programs, products, and services is given only casual attention. Even though the evaluation comes after the planning, assessment, and implementation stages, decisions about what is to be evaluated, who will be doing the evaluation, the manner in which the evaluation is to occur, and finally, the uses for information obtained in the evaluation process need to be made prior to the assessment and implementation stages.

USES OF EVALUATION

For what purposes can we use the data (information) we collect to evaluate our health promotion programs? We have listed some of of these below.

1. To create a greater sense of accountability. This is the most common--and many believe most important--use of evaluation at all program levels.

2. To assist with program planning and development

3. To help program personnel to systematically examine what is working and what isn't.

4. To assist with program development

5. To disseminate information about how the program should and is working.

THE TWO MAIN ROLES EVALUATIONS CAN PLAY

Formative Evaluation: The continuous and informal process of reassessing and improving ongoing program activities. Most health promotion planners keep some of these records. Examples of these evaluation measures include the following:

1.   Number of programs offered
2.   Number of participants
3.   Selection of program topics
4.   Feedback from group leaders and instructors
5.   Opinions and feedback of participants

LEVELS OF EVALUATION

The following three levels of evaluation are usually not implemented at the same time in the evaluation effort. We consider them to provide you with a sense of the range of possibilities in the evaluation process. As Moberg (1984) explains, *evaluation is not a single method, design, or approach, but a smorgasbord from which to pick and choose as appropriate to accountability requirement, your information needs, and the available resources.*

The Process Level: The inputs and activities of the program itself are considered. This is useful for formative evaluation, describing staff and participant characteristics, interactions, and transactions; for understanding the program's theory; for needs assessment; and for detailed description and documentation of the services actually rendered.

Process data is useful both in day-to-day management and planning activity, and in disseminating a program model for possible implementation or replication at another site. Process evaluation often focuses on effort, regardless of output or effectiveness. This level is basically the same as formative evaluation.

How many employees actually enrolled in the smoking cessation program? How does the number of enrollees relate to the number who originally said they wanted to attend? How many enrollees liked the program?

Outcome Evaluation: This level examines the attainment of program objectives related to short-and long-term change in participants' behavior, attitudes, or knowledge. Attaining satisfactory outcomes is the primary or ultimate reason that programs are established, and thus deserves attention in most efforts at program evaluation. The smoking cessation program would have a successful outcome if a meaningful percentage of participants did not begin to smoke in the near future.

Efficiency may also be looked at as part of an outcome study. This involves the consideration of alternative strategies for minimizing costs while maximizing outcome. Could the same level of outcome be accomplished at less cost in terms of money, time, personnel, and participant time, energy, and inconvenience? Cost-benefit and cost-effectiveness research measure program efficiency. What is the ratio of monetary return the organization can expect as a result of the smoking cessation program? Is it truly cost effective to conduct this program on-site?

Impact Evaluation: This level refers to the assessment of longer term, generalized results of program operation. This relates to the organizational needs and problems which led to the establishment of the program. Impact evaluation helps to ascertain whether the total effect of the program has been beneficial. The key difference between outcome and impact evaluation is that outcome considers only the direct program participants, while impact is concerned with the target population.

Has the outcome of this program helped further the organizational objectives of: 1) providing a smoke-free work environment for our employees; and 2) reducing organizational health care costs?

Additional Considerations in Designing Evaluation Studies

The task of program evaluation can be difficult for those inexperienced in instrument design and statistical analysis. Many health promotion coordinators will find it useful to seek the advise and/or involvement of experts in this area to complete complex evaluation studies. The following are often used as guidelines by competent researchers when conducting these studies:

1.   **Clarity**--Is the purpose clearly understood and articulated prior to the onset of the evaluation process? Having unambiguously phrased hypotheses should provide this clarity.

2.   **Validity**--Does the study evaluate what was intended? If we are measuring the effect of a fitness program on health care resource utilization patterns, have we controlled for the fact that the healthiest employees are the most likely to enroll.

3.   **Reliability**--Do the measurements used provide accurate information? How reliable is the Center for Disease Control Health Risk Appraisal in predicting risk factors for early death and disease?

4.   **Objectivity**--Are the interpretations of the findings consistent among multiple observers?

The organizational (particularly corporate) environment is not the ideal research setting. Often biases and other considerations, i.e., conflict with other corporate objectives, will displace objective interpretations.

5.   **Need**--Does the scope of the evaluation meet its intended need? Is it over or under-designed? In a study to determine the effect of a smoking cessation program on health costs over time, your study would be under-designed if you had to rely on only the

memory of the individual participants to provide data on health care utilization. You need access to the health claims records.

6. Credibility--Will the outcomes of the evaluation be used in making program decisions? This is partly a people issue. Often, because of politics or other organizational considerations, program changes indicated by the evaluation simply will not be implemented, or at least in an optimum time frame.

CONCLUSION: THREE REASONS WHY HEALTH PROMOTION PROGRAMS FAIL

Often, workplace health promotion programs are created, implemented and evaluated without proper consideration of emerging social issues. Some programs will likely fai,l and have failed, simply because they have not addressed this changing work ethic. It is important to examine why health promotion programs fail so that we may learn from such mistakes.

1. Organizational Problems

These are problems outside the control, but not the influence of employees. These problems are caused primarily by insufficient job design, improper work tasks, lack of supervision, insufficient administration, inadequate training, lack of career development, lack of power, or lack of authority.

2. Program Problems

These problems relate to the planning, design, and implementation of the program.

3. People Problems

These problems relate to the nature of program support by top management, the values and norms in the organizational climate, support among participants for the program, degree of interpersonal conflict in the organization, and competency of program facilitators.

8

THE LEADERSHIP CHALLENGE: MANAGING CULTURE

INTRODUCTION: WHAT IS EFFECTIVE LEADERSHIP

Leadership is the art and science of getting things done through people. Leaders are those key individuals who must face both outward to read the signs of pivotal changes and trends around them and face inward to empower and energize the organization, management and all employees with vision and purpose. Burns(1978:18) has defined leadership in the following way:

When persons with certain motives and purposes mobilize, in competition or conflict with others, institutional, political, psychological, and other resources so as to arouse, engage, and satisfy the motives of followers.

Leadership is the heart and blood of any organization: it pumps vitality into the task and team processes of reading and responding to the challenges that rapid change requires. Leaders, are more than managers. They must set the organizational direction with clear purposes and mobilize organizational resources for attaining often divergent goals. Good leaders manage through their follower's point of view (Zierden, 1980:27).

Leadership is this view process of gaining our commitment and cooperation, moving various teams or organizational units into action and making sure that team talents and potentials are fully utilized. The effective leader knows how build morale through this surfacing of latent   group talent or underutilized skills. Leadership is certainly important for accomplishing job tasks not just pointing us in the right direction; but visionary enthusiasm, not dominance and control, is the essential driving force.

Effective leaders are able to identify the purposes and motives of employees in a way that also allows them to tie their personal goals with the organizations more abstract mission or purpose. This process is also a great morale builder. Leaders inspire, motivate and leave workers with the feelings of being understood and cared about. Many good leaders are also good managers and they can effectively function in the trenches when they need to.

Leaders create a climate of competence and purpose; they inspire our best efforts. They make us feel confident we are moving in the right direction and we begin to enthusiastically look forward to new challenges and opportunities. They have great powers of imagination and tap a deep pool of experience with a keen sense of timing. They know their professional fields of expertise, yet appear humble as they draw upon diverse sources of information to identify and act decisively upon strategic targets of opportunity. They revitalize both organizations and employees.

The leader must always think and act proactively. This mindset demands that leaders: look to the future for creative opportunities: that nurture entrepreneurs and innovators as well as workhorses; that feedforword data and ideas for the future, not just feedback rewards for previous success; that can turn any setback into a positive learning opportunity.

The higher one goes in the organization, the more latitude exists for leading. However, the good leader knows that power is two-way street. Freedom to control is never without limits; it is always constrained by the actions of followers, a resource base, stakeholder interests, external trends and fluctuating environmental demands. To understand how to lead from the followers viewpoint, requires a good amount of self-esteem, awareness of one's strengths and weaknesses, and confidence that the talent exists within the organization, or through recruiting, to meet the challenges of change.

A BRIEF DETOUR INTO THE RESEARCH

The traditional model of group leadership (Bales, 1950) utilizes two factors, task direction and socioemotional support   Halpern and Winer call them initiating structure and consideration.   Effective group leaders must tap the resources of their groups to achieve both emotional support and task accomplishment.   Halpern and Winer found that although superiors thought that the best crew leaders were strong in initiating structure, the group members themselves believed that the best leaders displayed equal use of both traits.

This research was expanded upon by Fiedler (1967; 1974) who added that your success depends upon the type of leadership you utilize in different situations and your ability to manage such contingent variables as the impact of the entire organization, the task structure (whether structured or ambiguous), power, the type of people working with you, and acceptance of the leader. Success is related to both leadership style and and opportunities (configuration of situational variables) provided the leader to exert influence His research indicated that task-orientated leaders generally do better than supportive leaders, when both leaders are acceptable to the group (has power, formal backing, well-structured tasks, and group is ready to be directed).   However, supportive leaders do better in situations of unstructured tasks and low power(situations of emergency, crisis, transition or lack of consensus).

Process or cognitive models (House, 1971; House and Dessler, 1974) emphasizes the following components:

1) Arousing subordinates controllable needs;
2) Structuring payoffs for goal attainment;
3) Coaching and direction goal, attainment payoff paths;
4) Assisting subordinates in clarifying the expectations by reducing frustration;
5) And increasing performance-linked opportunities for personal satisfaction.

Oldham's (1976) model links leadership through work or task activities to motivation. Good leaders use motivational strategies that link task to valued positive outcomes for the individual. Strategies include: allowing personally rewarding tasks; setting goals; building feedback mechanisms; designing meaningful and fair reward systems; designing well defined and clear expectations into various job categories; promoting for performance and placing those individuals in rewarding jobs; penalizing poor performance in ways that encourage the possibility for improvement. This model focuses on the actual behavior of managers, rather than their leadership style.

Here are some factors that influence the practice of effective leadership:

1) Understands manager's and suborinates' history, values, goals.
2) Perceives with great insight the external environment.
3) Knows the attributes of top managers and important em-ployees.
4) Understands quite well the task requirements of key pos-itions in the organization.
5) Understands and utilizes the organizational culture or climate.
6) Knows how to design organizational structures to maxi-mize its effectiveness.

CONTEMPORARY LEADERSHIP MODELS: WHICH SKILLS COUNT?

Bennis (1983) and Bennis and Nanus (1985) have defined the art form of leadership and its transformative power as residing in three components: the leader (self-management), how the leader expresses his or her compelling vision and the organization. The key skills that the leader must have are the following:

1. **Vision:** the capacity to create and communicate a compelling vision or a desired state of affairs - to impart clarity to

this vision (or paradigm, context, frame) and induce commitment to it.

2. Communication and alignment: the capacity to communicate the vision in order to gain the support of their multiple constituencies.

3. Focus: the capacity to maintain the organization's direction, especially when the going gets rough.

4. Empowerment: the capacity to create environments(the appropriate social architecture) that can tap and harness the energies and abilities necessary to bring about results.

5. Organizational learning and education: the capacity to find ways for the organization to monitor its own performance, compare results with established objectives, have access to a continuously evolving data base on which to review past actions and base future ones, and decide how, if necessary, the organizational structure and the key personnel must be abandoned or rearranged when faced with new conditions (Bennis, 1983:18).

Finally, every leader must be aware of four dimensions or organization/structure:

1) **The manifest organization:** the one seen on the organization chart and formally displayed.
2) **The assumed organization:** the one that individuals perceive as the organization.
3) **The extant organization:** the organization as revealed through systematic investigations.
4) **The requisite organization:** the organization as it will be, if it were in accord with the reality of the situation within which it exists (Bennis, 1983:21-22).

Bennis and Nanus completed a study of (1985) 90 top leaders in American society which supports the importance of characteristics, like a compelling vision, clarity of goal direction and a conscientious use of time.   The four characteristics associated with leaders who truly inspire and care for their work are:

       1. A sense of significance and feeling that they make a contribution to how the world is built.

       2. A sense of learning the mastery of competence where the work force becomes a supergraduate school.

       3. A sense of community, college, or some shared affinity in working on a joint project or common cause.

       4. A sense of excitement and fun - of enjoyment in going to work everyday (Bisesi, 1983:46).

Bisesi (1983:62) lists two main characteristics of a successful leader as follows:

       He or she must view **1)** an organization as part of a total system; and he or she must **2)** cultivate people as the most important resource of the organization.

As we have already seen, leaders focus on doing the right things: they have a compelling vision, a dream about their tasks. Leaders seldom waste time because they are busy creating the artful leadership style which means taking a more holistic and environmentally open viewpoint: they constantly scan the external world for pivotal events, opportunities and trends that the organization must manage.

Effective leaders are successful because they know how to use the skills of communication, motivation, participation and empowerment to mobilize organizational resources to achieve worthy cultural values and productive business relationships. Good leadership manages proactively through enabling structures, rewards and resources which encourage participation for innovation and customer or client focus It is forward looking because it allows innovative people with a proven track record to utilize the long-term resources necessary to attempt risky projects, instead of seeking short-term rewards for tasks already complete. Once again we see the power of forward looking visions.

An effective leader must be able to use organizational processes to achieve cultural values such as: 1) be willing to negotiate often through informal networks to accomplish goals; 2) have a heightened sense of corporate social responsibility; 3) be willing to give up authority through productive delegation; 4) take greater social responsibility for the career development of his or her people. Effective leadership is nurtured by adapting several key strategies, according to Bisesi (1983:63):

- learn more about people and how they work in groups and organizations;

- talk with people about their careers;

- hire broadly educated people;

- don't become obsolete - or at worse, dull;

- keep a low profile

Effective organizational leaders have the broad skill and perspective that supports more investment for training, educating, monitoring and coaching the next generation of leaders and managers. This process can assist us in the strategic task of individual renewal and organization revitalization. This task is based upon negotiating from a position of proactive vision through various means: empowering, communicating, motivating, participation, teamwork and, ultimately, organizational innovation.

The task in an even broader sense concerned with the long-term promotion of societal leadership and a new national competitive agenda for merging productivity and the quality of life in the 21st Century. This process is one of promoting transformation leadership (Burns, 1978) which sets the value patterns for our entire society. The task is one of establishing the vision of a human resource society which places the importance of people as our most productive and important assets on a level with all the strategic considerations.

The proactive approach begins with the understanding and revitalization of oneself, of others, of tasks, teams, situations and the entire organization. It is instructive to review the study by McCall and Lombardo (1983) where senior executives rank ordered, beginning with the most frequently mentioned negative reasons first, that executives career paths were derailed:

1) Insensitive to others: abrasive, intimidating, bullying style;
2) Cold, aloof, arrogant;
3) Betrayal of trust;
4) Overly ambitious: thinking of next job,playing politics de structively;
5) Specific performance problems with the business;
6) Overmanaging: unable to delegate or build effective work groups or teams;
7) Unable to staff effectively;
8) unable to think and act strategically;
9) Unable to adapt to a boss with a different style;
10) Overdependent on advocate or mentor.

The three lessons from this research and other sources are quite clear. **First,** as an effective leader you must know yourself and your strengths and weaknesses. **Second**, you must know the parameters of the situations you face, including individual talent, tasks, and teams. this might include knowing where you are going(vision), how you are getting there(structure of team), expectations for team members(targets, standards of performance) and how to encourage team spirit and involvement(good communication flow among all members,informal meetings and discussions, resolving unnecessary conflicts promptly, and being very approachable). **Third**, you must try to match your leadership style with situations in a flexible way.

CULTURE AND LEADERSHIP

Our daily work lives are intimately cultural bound and shaped. Culture unconsciously permeates the very processes of our perception of work relations and molds our view of the entire world. Culture is the deepest layer of organizational meaning and processes and leaders need to become intimate with its increasing importance as they attempt to renew or revitalize their organizations.

Each organization has its own unique culture or way of doing things. Just like the larger society, it also has subcultural groups that produce contradictory values and norms. Leadership is often faced with the task of turning this diversity to the organizations advantage. No organization functions without diverse subsystem values in tension. In fact, such conflicts, if properly managed, can increase organizational energy, vitality and success.

DEFINING ORGANIZATIONAL CULTURE

Organizational or corporate culture can be defined by focusing upon its components: myths, rituals, stories, sagas, ceremony, humor, symbols, values and language. Cohen et al (1980:337) writing in the tradition of organizational behavior defines organizational culture as:

> the customary way of doing things, attitude values that are 'in the air' affecting everyone. The organization's attitude about authority how it should be used, interpersonal style, conflicts and so forth which condition and affect all other changes.

Van Manen and Schein (1978: 1) define organizational culture as:

> longstanding rules of thumb, a somewhat special language and ideology that helps edit a member's everyday (work) experience, shared standards of relevance as to the critical aspects of work. Matter of fact prejudices, models for social etiquette and demeanor, certain customs and rituals and a sort of residual category of some rather plain 'horse sense' regarding what is appropriate and 'smart' behavior within the organization and what is not.

Smirchich (1983:161) defines culture as the sense of coherence and-loyalty derived from social interactions and a shared meaning system:

> Widely shared interpretations of an organization's history, traditions, or goals and values, for example, may be used to provide a

source of coherence. To experience this allows our sources of identification to develop, thus binding individual and group.

Organizational culture promotes meaning and commitment in our daily work lives. It is acquired through observation, instruction and the desire to belong; its medium of expression is language, symbolism, and that cluster of processes we call socialization or enculturation. Both the cohesion and lubrication essential for building organized work life are sustained through the structuring activities that culture provides; they provide the foundation for purpose, meaning and a good measure of vital disagreement.

Organizational culture is also one of the engines for change and innovation. Culture can also become an impediment to needed changes when change is not aligned with it. Through culture some paradoxes of organizational life are revealed: between our desire for our organizations be a good and decent place to work and the realities of how it sometimes operates.

The reconciliation of such contradictions resides in how effective leaders are when establishing a clear direction for the organization and mobilizing support for it. Effective leaders know how to build commitment through clarity of purpose. This provides the organization a reason for doing business and sustains it through its plan or blueprint of priorities. It establishes and sanctions the values, principles and policy standards which guide the organization's business plans, management tasks, human resource activities, and structure for organizing work.

Successful leaders are able to give their organizations a clear vision and sense of purpose, which inspires all personnel toward high performance and meaningful goal attainment, even in the face of normal conflicts. They know how to use culture and tradition to provide a context for assuring the employees, stakeholders and other supporters that meaningful work is effectively performed, high quality product are created, and responsibility to standards of ethics and social responsibility are maintained.

Commitment is the human resource side of culture. Commitment to organizational goals will improve if leaders take the time to involve their workers in establishing and maintaining an organizational direction and purpose that members can truly identify with and care about achieving. It is through this clearly articulated and communicated vision that proactive leadership earns its credibility.

ORGANIZATIONAL CULTURAL MANAGEMENT

Reactive leadership ignores managing cultural issues pertaining to organizational purpose and direction. Some people believe that culture is too deep to be managed at the surface. I disagree ,once we accept some limitations.

Cultural management is the process of not only developing the ultimate purposes and aims of the organization but, also, providing value-based formulations of mission, objectives, goals and strategies for reaching them. It does this while promoting a sense of shared expectation and appropriate behavior. A statement of organizational purpose or mission should address such fundamental strategic questions as: why does this organization exist? What are we committed to? What about this organization is different from other organizations in our competitive environment?

Deal and Kennedy (1982:16) speak of promoting a strong organizational culture. A strong culture is a system of information about how people are to behave most of the time. By knowing in what direction the organization is headed and exactly what is expected of them to help the organization to reach its goals, employees waste little time deciding how to act in a given situation. A strong culture enables people to feel better about what they do, so they are more likely to work smarter and harder. Strong culture companies remove a great deal of uncertainty because they provide the assumptions, rationale, structure, standards, and value systems which we know will consistently provide clear guidelines.

Such a strong culture is often embodied in its leadership and management philosophy and style. Effective cultural values need to be clearly articulated and communicated by managers, as well as leaders, and understood by employees throughout the organization. This process is accomplished through the competent human relations skills of its leaders and managers, and the assistance of human resource staff. The benefits of bringing organizational cultural clarity into line management philosophy and behavior is articulated by Albert and Silverman (1984:13) with the following results:

(1) greater commitment to the organization's objectives, notably quality, good customer service, high productivity, and so on; (2) increased employee effort, pride and loyalty; (3) lower turnover; (4) faster implementation of plans, projects, and programs; (5) more effective problem solving at all organizational levels; and (6) the ability to grow rapidly through directing more effort towards implementing plans, programs and objectives, and less effort towards fighting fires, plugging holes, and constantly resolving conflicts about how things should be done around here.

Deal and Kennedy (1982:31), also, point out several positive outcomes of shared values and beliefs that supports more innovative and responsive organizational structures and processes. Values determine paths for successful career mobility. They communicate to the community, the consumer, and the outside world the organization's ethical standards, strategic purposes, and expectations of quality (Deal and Kennedy, 1982:33).

Different organizational cultures lend support for different structural arrangements and leadership/managerial styles of interaction. An understanding of the cultural context is crucial for assessing the meaning of managerial performance and organizational effectiveness. Also, cultural issues frame how the organization perceives its problems; the pathways for seeking and using power; how to obtain resources/assistance; how to gain rewards; and finally, how the organization views creativity, innovation, and work quality.

The topic of organizational culture should not become reduced to a simple panacea for all organizational problems. For example, we have little scholarly evidence linking culture to financial performance measures. By over-emphasizing the uses of cultural factors, we tend to ignore the role of size, technology, market position, environmental influences, resource limitations, financial controls, marketing expertise, product development strategies, and government policy.

The corporate cultural metaphor permits us to ask empirical questions and seek relationships we might have overlooked using other perspectives. For example, it provides a different perspective or lens for viewing organizational problems by exploring issues, like the expressive dimensions of work behavior, how informal relations makes work more interesting, and how organizations can become an unconscious breeding ground for conflicts.

We must remember than when we are using metaphors the idea of verification of knowledge is put in the background. The essence of metaphor is the attempt to experience and understand two divergent things relative to each another. Cultural language and ritual provides us metaphorical tools that can guide our search for more creative and innovative solutions to organizational problems and issues.

Organizations can utilize symbolic and ritual activities to explore issues of cultural renewal and transformation. This may happen at ceremonies, recognition events, stockholder meetings, company picnics, speak-up breakfasts, graduation events or any rite of passage for employees, clients or participants in organizations. Our literal concepts may sometimes only represent a partial, abbreviated view of the complexity before us. Wonder and humility are essential ingredients of any liberally educated and caring leader. As William James (1890:288-289) once framed the issue of learning in artistic terms:

The mind is at every stage a theater of simultaneous possibilities. the mind, in short, works on the data it receives very much as a sculptor works on his block of stone. In a sense, the statue stood there from eternity.But there were a thousand different ones beside it, and the sculptor alone is to thank for having extracted this one from the rest.

LEADING AND MANAGING TEAMS AND GROUPS

The importance of leading and managing various types of group processes is primary. The very idea of an organization or business is nothing more than an integrated and coordinated series of processes in various systems aimed at changing something that is lacking or only partially useful (design feature) into something fully useful (finished product has a benefit). Of course, consumer, customer and and client response will determine the degree of our product/service design and marketing success. Virtually every system, leadership and management function manipulates processes through some form of group interaction.

Processes are intimately tied with both group effectiveness and change itself. The transformations (another word for process) occurring in systems through various forms of managed group activity add value to the primary inputs or resources. Anything can serve as the raw material for this conversion process (what we have), but not anything can become a successful product or service (what someone else wants or needs). It is through change in processes that expectation is converted into meaningful results.

Successful efforts are based upon effective leaders and managers: the former guiding the purpose and direction of processes and deciding how and what value(benefits, quality, resources) will be added; and the latter managing or effectively organizing, planning, coordinating controlling these efforts through team or group work. This is why leadership and management are so important: without purpose, direction and management skills guiding programs or work processes, they will not produce quality or valuable results; only wasted motion and nonessential activity. And this latter type of result is not the only one that counts. Activity is not itself productive, unless it is a necessary component of a viable and valued process.

How we deal with people in group situations is one strategic clue to leading, managing and developing effective employees. One of the best ways to manage the impacts of change upon work (conversion) processes is to utilize flexible work groups or teams. Realizing the challenges that discontinuous change creates for any organization, we begin to understand the value of a well educated, innovative, and adaptable work group. The key process vulnerabilities in this change dominated, high-technology, information age, are the excessive use of mechanical, non adaptable, rigid, routine and inflexible processes for managing work and the people responsible for its effective performance .

The last assertion is not a criticism of the use of computers or its application to the drudge jobs of industry. However, we must not try to program the people doing the programming (leading, managing or working). We can't "hard wire" all the alternatives into a model of effective work, but we can use the model as an ingenious device to give us parameters for judging different alternatives.

We must, in fact, finally rely upon human judgment and the contributions of team members to think and work productively together, under increasingly variable conditions. Some of these conditions include: more decentralized and flatter organizational structures; self-managed work teams; more management participation and delegation; new demands for flexible, precise and tailored information; more direct, yet informal observation of work process by leaders and consultants; more built in redundancy (provides alternatives) in manufacturing (buy it, make it, switch lines, make it here assemble it elsewhere); more flexible production lines and more measurements of quality built into the work process).

So many daily work functions are built into group activities that we need to understand more precisely what helps groups to work more productively(become a team) and what detracts them from being effective. This discussion will only focus on teams and why they fail and how to improve team effectiveness(see Gutknecht and Miller, 1986:133-151, for a more general discussion of literature regarding group dynamics). But first let's spend time on some **action ideas** for facilitating any group.

THE 3 M'S OF FACILITATING A GROUP.

1. MOBILIZING: (Moving the Group) The leader begins a didactic exercise by saying something like' "I'd like to begin our group (class, workshop,meeting) today of   "Overeater's Anonymous" by asking each of you to describe how you feel when you are 15 lbs over your desired weight. This type of technique is a catalyst to get the group mobilized, or moving in a specific mode or direction.

2. MANAGING: (Directing the Group) The leader asks members to observe any one of number of simple communication techniques when they speak out such as:

> Realize the various uses for asking questions--persuade, plant ideas, clear up thinking,motivate, problem solve,take the sting out of criticism, overcoming objection, gaining cooperation, are reducing mistakes, stem anxiety, and defuse a volatile situa tion;

> Using an I Message when they speak such as "I feel.........";

> Listen for total meaning;

> Respond to feelings;

> Note all cues;

> Observe barriers to communication;
> Use questions that are either specific to clear up a point of fact or open-ended to thought and encourage continued explore ation.

3. MODELING: (Leading by example)-- The leader shows the group members how to communicate in the group by his/her personal example. He comments using "I" Messages, and directing comments to other members while maintaining eye contact.

This model is a very simple working model for building a successful group in an organizational setting. Any classroom, work setting or group can become a laboratory in skill acquisition. In a very real sense, this is a model of training and teaching in that it utilizes telling, showing, and doing as strategies for conveying skills, information and learning.

STRATEGIES FOR WORKING WITH GROUPS

These simple **action strategies** can be utilized by any teacher or training instructor to insure that the students will be able to grasp and absorb the material presented. They are especially helpful trying to make learning a diverse and exciting group process.

1. PRESENTING INFORMATION: (TELLING)

* Explain only the major points and concepts needed for the learners to apply a new skill.

* Use a variety of presentation methods NOTE: (Never lecture for more than 15 minutes at a time.)

2. GIVING DEMONSTRATIONS: (SHOWING)

* If a skill or information is complex, it is important for the instructor to show each part of the idea or behavior relates to the entire concept or picture.

* If possible, let a class participant demonstrate. their new learning or skill behavior with other members of the group.

* Use a video of the person presenting the material or practicing the skill correctly (If available)

* Follow demonstrations as soon as possible with additional practice opportunities in dyads or the entire class.

3. EXPERIENTIAL OPPORTUNITIES: (DOING)
* Use Role Playing exercises whenever possible.

As the two individuals perform, others in the class can mentally learn by recognizing the correct application. Ask other members of the class to give feedback concerning how the exercise was performed, and then reverse the roles and parts as frequently as possible.

TEAMS VERSUS GROUPS

Groups exhibit certain traits which sometimes get in the way of effective team building. First, groups tend to overemphasize current goals, at the expense of what they might ultimately accomplish as a team. Second, they are often more reactive and go along with the crowd and more prone to groupthink; while teams are more proactive, which allows the contribution of each unique personality, and actually inspires mutual vision, energy, and support. Third, groups involve people only in limited ways, and see participation as questioning of authority; while teams want people to get involved and committed and see problem solving as opportunity for mutual contribution, because they practice joint ownership of problems.

Fourth and finally, groups sometimes overcontrol information, resist disagreement and emphasize personal convenience over group agreement. This creates the common problem of implementing any solution to a problem. In contrast, effective teams communicate fully and openly, share information, try to recognize both individual and group contributions, proactively mediate conflicts before they become destructive, and keep the commitments that they all agreed upon.

LEADERSHIP, POWER, AND TEAM EFFECTIVENESS

Pfeffer (1981:7) sees power as "a property of systems at rest; politics is the study of power in action". Brym (1980:26) defines power as "the structurally determined capacity to control others by deciding issues, by deciding which issues are to be contentious, and by suppressing manifest and latent conflicts". Power includes both the ability to initiate action and to resist or stop activity. In contrast, power in action is politics: the action side of organizational bargaining for resources (Lukes, 1976).

The negative or destructive uses of power creates destructive resistance. All uses of power probably create some resistance. Resistance cannot be avoided. In fact, it is a sign of healthy involvement. It signals the need to recognize that involved and regarded workers can be trusted and are often more productive than those who are, or feel, excluded from meaningful involvement in the decision making process.

Power of necessity involves some bargaining over organizational resources, such as position, information, access, and coalition membership. Successful leaders recognize the reality of conflict over resources and know how to use resources to build effective work teams and mitigate negative or destructive resistance. This team conflict model recognizes that consensus is not always possible, or even healthy for the organization, and that attempts to avoid worker participation, bargaining, or resistance can lead to negative secondary effects, such as worker passivity, alienation, and destructive, covert resistance. These effects, in turn, can contribute to the deterioration of managerial legitimacy, a decrease in morale and productivity, and increased absenteeism and turnover.

The effective use of teams by enlightened leadership can eliminate unnecessary conflicts through the proper exercise of power on a human scale. The fight against arbitrary power is a constant struggle because it is easy to fall into the trap of converting power into such metaphorical security blankets as paternalism or workaholic control: "management always knows best." Effective leaders use cultural visions and values, to create a climate supportive of learning, collaboration, innovation and employee development. Effective leaders know that investments in productive people and teams create the groundwork for productive organizations.

If organizations are to proactively resolve their problems, and if both organizations and employees are to achieve their true potential, both must revise their understanding of power. Power cannot be treated as the sole possession of either management or employees. Instead, it must be defined as a negotiated relationship between people. In ignoring this relationship, managers downplay their dependence on employees and use power coercively and destructively (Knight and Roberts, 1982:47-61).

The essential point is that power or legitimate authority has two sides: a dominating side and a participatory side. Power as legitimate authority recognizes the need for constructive bargaining; hence, it transforms covert resistance into working agreements, working arrangements, compromises, and sometimes even tolerable opposition. Thus, the negative and destructive effects of denying participation can be changed into a more rational view: conflict may be organized, managed, and dealt with through bargaining, participation, shared respect and the spirit of compromise; or effectively reduced(some say coopted) through an adequate investment in human resources and effective organizational programs and systems.

This view is compatible with both our emphasis on work teams and human resource strategies; which call for recognizing the interests, skills, motivations and values of organizational members at all levels. This process not only empowers the worker but it energizes the entire organization.

Burke (1982:134) makes the same general argument for consultants for consultants: "The consultant should help the client empower his or her subordinates so that their energy can be channeled toward team and organizational achievements rather than toward passive hostility, inappropriate competitiveness and an overdependence on rules or feelings of powerlessness." Burke sees the need for consultants to understand the role of power in effectively managed organizations.

CONCLUSIONS

Leadership is the art and science of getting things done through people.   The leader must always think and act proactively.   Effective leaders are able to identify the purposes and motives of employees in a way that also allows them to tie their personal goals with the organizations more abstract mission or purpose. Effective leaders are also able to use power constructively to mobilize resources to creatively and constructively meet the challenges of change.   They invest those resources in promising future trends and opportunities: including education, training, new technologies and new ways of managing and using vital information.   They know how to build a responsive and forward looking corporate culture that rewards results, quality, and excellence, wherever it is found, from boardroom to laundry- room.

9

HUMAN RESOURCES:
MEETING THE CHALLENGES OF CHANGE

INTRODUCTION

In today's turbulent environment, the issue is how to create more adaptable, flexible, creative and productive employees and organizations. In this view, the daily internal management of task processes must not become separated from strategic and creative thinking about pivotal external changes and trends.

In light of the tremendous pace of change, the strategic revitalization and renewal of both workers and organizations can no longer be thought of as a luxury. We need to educate everyone to think smarter and for leadership to think strategically.

FROM STRATEGIC PLANNING TO ORGANIZATIONAL REVITALIZATION

Strategic planning asks questions about our current line of business: What we should be doing; in what direction we should be going? Strategic planning allows the organization to clarify goals, values and culture; define the mission or purpose; and creatively examine the external environment, devoid of rush. It must be comprehensive, open, honest and imaginative. It also must systematically outline the strategies, products, directions, interventions, programs, management skills and information needs that will allow us to meet our business objectives. This analysis produces a strategic thrust for the organization.

Robbins (Robbins, 1983) contrasts strategic planning with a more evolutionary mode of strategy formulation. The former explores the current situation in order to formulate a well planned set of guidelines for achieving where one wants to go. The latter model is not systematic or well thought out; it evolves "as a pattern or a stream of significant decisions." The evolutionary model has been gaining some favor of late because it includes dimensions that are more dynamic and flexible. Some like to use the words chaotic, unpredicable or paradoxical.

Evolutionary, ecological, resource dependency and population models fit within this latter tradition (Robbins, 1983). In this perspective, the complex external environment sets the stage for adjustment or coping behavior. It shapes organizational structure, rather than letting strategy determine structure, as is the case in the planning view. Thus, excessive confidence in rational strategy is downplayed. Although there are numerous differences in the reource adaptation and evolutionary models, the important point is that the organizations can not always control, plan or respond to rapid change by trusting only top-down, planning solutions.

The literature on strategic planning, is often guided by deterministic life cycle assumptions. Many companies believe product lines will always follow natural life cycles of growth and decline. The problem with such views resides in their deterministic, biological assumptions. Maturity, growth and decline are not inevitable; nor are they incapable of extension through renewal and revitalization. Any business or organizational unit can experience life cycle revitalization, rejuvenation, and extension through active self-examination.

An example from the Japanese will highlight this contention. Why did many Japanese electronic companies not eliminate the radio as a viable product just because it seemed to lag behind its technological potential? The answer lies in how the Japanese define their products. Instead of defining them in a narrow manner as a declining product, or a cash dog in the sunset of its life cycle, the Japanese defined this produt in a broader way. For example the product concept of a radio was enlarged to include more exciting technological design possibilities in an interactive media age. Of course, the Japanese continue to invest money exploring the potential of these new product lines. The very successful walkman, watchman video(video wrist-watch) and digital tape are but three excellent examples.

Many organizations are today displaying the same innovative and creative thinking that prompted some Japanese companies to allow their products follow a more evoluntionary path. Thus, they have not followed an inevitable cycle to decline. Today, many are functioning profit centers created through the extension and redefinition of prevoius ly successful products and the long-term belief intechnology.

Traditional, strategic planning is still a valuable tool in the arsenal of strategic management. However, its failures result from its narrow emphasis upon traditional tools such as corporate portfolio management, narrow return on investment assumptions, management by numbers, mergers and paper entrepreneurism (Reich, 1983).

Good strategists exercise entrepreneurial, energizing and futuristic skills. They review targets, resources and those things worth doing, with as little waste as possible. They actively experiment and learn to anticipate problems and trends by asking questions regarding market segments, customers and their organizational vision, mission and business plan.

Formal strategic planning mechanisms don't provide the certainty that leadership will focus upon the right things in a complex and changing world. New environmental forces, stakeholders, assumptions, products, market segments, competitors, opportunities and threats must be constantly monitored. Organizations must devote continuous effort to strategic thinking, human resource development, active learning, and flexible, futures planning. The process and the outcome are both highly strategic for survival.

Organizations today must systematically evaluate important trends anticipate strategic issues, while exploring options. Environmental scanning, trend analysis, and issues anticipation are useful tools for building more proactive agendas for the future. Building scenarios of the future (like the process of modeling) assists the organization to gain clarity and to plan for alternative strategic responses to various trend options. Which brings us back to the topic of human resources and the quality of people assisting us in this process. Instead of attempting these tasks on a grand scale and in a completely separate planning or HR department, they should become part of a smaller scale staff effort, integrated with quality control, new technological and information processes, entrepreneurial values and creativity and innovation concerning the needs of line management.

UTILIZING HUMAN RESOURCES EFFECTIVELY

Chalofsky and Lincoln (1983:16-19) suggest that the field of human resource development can be analyzed in five ways: (1) *conceptual/philosophical*--the development of human potential or helping people grow; (2) *operational*--changing behavior through learning and training; (3) *functional* --executive development, career counseling, internal consulting, and sales training; (4) *field of practice*--occupation such as learning consultant or career counseler; (5) *field of study*--such as sociology, education, counseling, management science, and psychology.

GROWTH OF HUMAN RESOURCE MANAGEMENT: FROM FUNCTION TO STRATEGY

The traditional view of the personnel or human resource management field is one of fragmentation. Many line managers think of the personnel's department responsibilities as a series of disjointed activities, such as compensation, benefits, labor relations, employee relations, training, organization development, staffing placement, orientations, performance appraisal, promotions, affirmative action, equal employment opportunity, and health and safety.

This view of fragmented HRM departmental functions is not far from the truth in many organizations. Personnel functions have often historically occupied separate departments; each develop their own guidelines, policies and implementation systems. These traditional personnel practices were not connected to the needs of line managers or organizational strategy.

Traditional personnel practices evolved in reaction to specific, historical problems and needs, rather than for proactive strategic reasons. Personnel departments were reactive because large organizations created them to address costly problems that emerged with a more complex socal and economic world: the bigger the organization, the more personnel functions. These more.complex organizations required a central administrative apparatus to recruit, follow legislative guidelines, bargain with more sophisticated unions, evaluate, reward, train and compensate a growing and more sophisticated work force.

New human resource functions have often evolved in a rather hit or miss fashion. When the need was great enough departments were added. For example, labor relations was added to deal with collective bargaining in complex unionized industries. Affirmative action and equal employment opportunity legislation encouraged the development of appropriate functions in personnel departments to handle compliance with government regulations. Thus, the modern human resource department evolved as a series of reactions to external events; disjointed activities and functions, lacking coherence and strategic focus, resulted.

The primary strategic tasks of human resource departments in today's competitive world are revitaliztion and renewal of people and organizational systems. The HR professional must learn to function as more than a mere staff adjunct. They must become more proactive and anticipate the practical needs of line management. Likewise, line managers must be able to ask and answer the right questions when confronted with HRM problems. HR professionals must be able to assist managers by helping them to attract, select, orientate, socialize, promote, compensate, motivate, develop, keep and/or terminate employees, consistent with standards of justice, business effectiveness and employee capabilities and needs. Such specialists must learn how to renew and revitalize all organizational systems and processes.

THE HUMAN RESOURCE CHALLENGES OF A CHANGING SOCIETY

Four factors which account for the growing recognition and importance of human resource management functions: 1) economic; 2) government regulation; 3) demographic; and 4) social, legal, and value complexity.

First, the economic shifts over the past twenty years have created a period of increasing competition, declining productivity, technological obsolescence and growing deficits in domestic accounts and in international trade. Reich (1983) addresses this issue of economic decline by suggesting the need for a more flexible system, responsive to new markets, technologies, workers and foreign competition. This revitalization of technological andf human capital is based upon the integration of workers into productive teams who identify and solve complex organizational problems:

> *This new organization of work necessarily will be more collaborative, participative and egalitarian than is high-volume, standardized production, for the simple reason that initiative, responsibility, and discretion must be so much more widely exercised with it* (Reich, 1983:246).

The shifts in the economy also involve the changing unions and labor markets. Increasing educated workers, in many organizational and industrial sectors, demand more programs for personal and career development. Many organizations are trying to increase worker motivation and potential by breaking down arbitrary and fragmented task responsibilities.

In fact, the growth of large scale organizations, high-volume, standardized production, and rigid, mechanical, bureaucratic control strategies, have increased the separation between managers, supervisors and lower-level people. The human resource response must recognize that all employees have needs for meaningful participation, fair and just compensation, job security and desire to achieve personally meaningful career goals.

Still, human resource professionals need to examine both differences and similarities among various employee groups. The assumptions of value, skill, and lifestyle differences among workers must be evaluated and tested in the workplace. Let's review here some data on the workforce.

Kerr (1979:IX-XII) has identified four main periods of labor force evolution in the U.S.: *first,* the influx of immigrants and rise of heavy industry around 1880; *second,* the large rural to urban migration beginning in the early decades of the 1900's and accelerating after WWI; *third,* the introduction of social controls and involvement by government and trade unions, which grew during the new deal through the 1960's; and *fourth,* the current period where "tasks have changed, and the indulgence of psychic satisfactions has increased" (Kerr, 1979:XIII).

This new cultural orientation includes two key dimensions: 1) personal self-fulfillment and 2) increasing educational attainment:

> *The penetration of new attitudes and expectations into different segments of the American economy varies greatly. It is deeper where the labor force is younger than where it is older. Where it is more educated than less educated, and thus also more in white-collar than in blue-collar occupations* (Kerr, 1979: ii).

The dimensions of worker discontent are complex and often difficult to accurately measure.. Work discontent is often overstated, if attitudinal measures are used; less discontent is evident when behavioral measures are used. Discontented workers are more evident during times of affluence, when they are more likely to quit their jobs. However, this action can be interpreted as a form of positive discontent, because workers feel enough optimism about the economy to explore alternative opportunities. In constrast, during times of economic difficulty employees seldom quit their jobs and report more positive attitudes about work on surveys. Studies indicate that levels of work discontent and job satisfaction have not changed much over the past 30 years, for managers and white collar workers, back and white men and women. White males have shown more variable discontent, particularly during those bursts of affluence and because of baby boom competition and the Viet Nam war (Gutknecht 1985).

Various labor market conditions, like a surplus of low skill laborers or a shortage of high skilled technical workers, demand more complex management responses. In tight labor markets, organizations need to offer more benefits and opportunities than they would otherwise offer, in order to attract and keep good workers.

The shortage of skilled blue-collar workers in the machine tool industry, nurses in hospitals and clerical help in all industries are recent examples. In such tight labor market sectors, organizations must consider innovative human resource strategies to recruit, pay, promote and retain workers through difficult business cycles. For example, a program of secure employment, traded for the promise not to strike, might enlist some skilled trade workers frightened by their emerging obsolence.

Unions have also influenced HR policies and procedures. Even the threat or unionization has stimulated new consideration of more innovative policies, programs and management practices. The growth of unions and their political influence has influenced government regulation with both positive and negative impacts upon organizations.

The political activity of unions has also influenced legislation in the areas of occupational health and safety, workman's compensation, minimum wage and affirmative action. This regulatory environment has greatly influenced the emergence of the HR departments. In addition, HR strategies must cope with the trend toward more complex international labor relations and training issues--new joint overseas ventures, expanding Pacific Rim trade, the European orientation to retirement, training and labor relations, and the exporting of domestic (US) work to foreign countries.

Third, demographic factors have greatly improved the emergence of human resource management policies. From 1946 when 3.6 million babies were born, through 1954-64 when over 4 million births a year were recorded, our society expanded by 75 million new members. The 1950's alone accounted for 40 million new arrivals. In 1940 there were only 11 million children under age five; by 1960 20 million children were under the age of four. By 1969, four out of ten people in the U.S. were under 20 years old (Jones, 1980:10-19). What social implications do these facts reveal?

First, we find more involvement by women, working mothers, and single mothers, than anytime in the past. At the same time that more women are working, surveys indicate higher reports of sex discrimination brought about by changing perceptions and rising expectations.

Second, we find fewer older workers and increased numbers of younger, more educated workers. In addition, worker disatisfaction, brought about by increases in education, haseven filtered into the blue collar workplace. These younger, more educated blue-collar workers have the highest level of dissatisfaction, as well as very different expectations about work (Gutknecht, 1985).

Third, blacks are gaining opportunities in managerial and white collar work, but the absolute increase is marginal. Black women are gaining positions at the lower and mid levels of service and white collar sectors, as well as in some professional and managerial ranks.

Motivating highly educated workers, when promotional opportunities have been reduced, will be a major human resource challenge in the future. As promotions slow, those in the middle ranks are being squeezed; these employees are remaining in the same jobs for longer time spans, which can create unrest and boredom for them. Many lower level supervisor and bottom level management positions were designed to be either temporary training or pass-through jobs. In the future, how many highly qualified and talented workers will spend 5 to 10 years in jobs intended to be mastered in 2 years?

Another major trend, potentially increasing organization tension and requiring a strategic HR response, is the demographics of an older workforce. The increasing lenght of a worker's life not only stretches the former time boundaries of their career, it also stimulates both opportunities and strain for managers and HR strategies.

The notion of a career span or normative work life is implicit today within many organization's employment policies. Workers are concerned with career and life satisfaction. How long we expect workers to work is related to societal demands, demographics, emplement and retirement policies, job requirements, career specialization and preparation requirements, and skill obsolescence. In many organizations, career values and organizational structures seem at loggerheads.

Kanter (1983) has criticized a shift to faster career paths because we inevitabily lose the advantage of finding more mature workers who know their jobs comprehensively. Too often, younger managers with the right sponsorship and technical knowledge, succeed or fail in relatively short spans of time. The organization then suffers a leadership vacuum at certain levels. The shift to "fast trackers" seems outdated already; less relevant for nurturing of the generalist skills needed to lead more decentralized and information driven organizations into the 1990's and beyond.

Fourth, we find changes in the social, legal and value dimensions of our increasingly complex and interdependent world. Today, the focus of renewing organizations is upon treating people as assets, and not merely variable costs, despite the failures of many schemes devoted to human resource accounting (Odiorne, 1984:3-68). The competitive international challenge has exerted pressure on organizations to recognize employees as valuable resources and assets in their own right (see chapter7).

Modern organizations give us the material and cultural resources to express ourselves and strive for a material state of existence that seemed only a short time ago unthinkable. Our middle class lifestyle is stlll envied around the world. We must not take these successes for granted. However, many organizational leaders often fail to see employee struggles, their calls for participation and involvement as a golden opportunity for sharing the responsibility and accountability for organizational success and failure.

Human resource development issues can energize, motivate and challenge all of us to become more than we have been, if we allow ourselves the opportunity to link both personal and collective goals. Putting energy and vision into our work environments can lead to increased personal performance and organizational productivity: a win-win opportunity.

HR policies and practices are not formed in a social/ economic vacuum. They are influenced by many trends already discussed , including the changing configuration of society and international commerce. Human resource personne, just like line-managers and leaders, must recognize these changing values, ideologies, legislation and administrative regulations.

STRATEGIC HUMAN RESOURCE PRACTICES

We can identify five important areas for the revitalization and renewal of organizations. First, organizations must increase their flexibility and competitiveness through practices like work subcontracting and outsourcing for component parts; create larger numbers of redundant production systems to give alternatives in the face of change; develop more flexible productiion lines with CAD and CAM processes; have multiple suppliers for areas of most startegic resource need or dependency; finally, set up an externaly focused management consulting, management development, training and process research divisions or departments that will function as profit centers.

Second, organizations need to be more innovative regarding job definitions and job assignments by encouraging and promoting job enlargement, participation and ownership. This might involve such areas of interest as: more exploratory job transfers; the creation of and assignment to more nonmanagement positions for advanced specialists; recognizing diversity of experience as the key basis of promotion; and more reliance by corporations on the liberally trained business student or general liberal arts major.

Third, organizations must learn how to manage long- run cultural and strategic change by supporting grass roots innovations and innovative leaders. This may invove such strategies as: more exposure outside the organization through extended leaves, sabbaticals trading and cross-training of personnel; more outside seminars, workshops and symposiums; manditory continuing education policy; broadening the use of interdisciplinary teams, task forces, and special project groups.

Fourth, the organization must learn to shift its focus from predetermined product features to a concern with customer benefits or use. This may require more of the following: the use of information surveys, questionaires and market tests; more management by walking around (MBWA), process observation, and just asking pertinent questions; more pilot studies, analyses, and programs; more customer audits; and more listening and communication training for executives.

Fifth, the organizations must move to a broader concern with the entire organizational environment, including human resource, marketing, information, technology, health promotion and external issues. Such areas of interest might include the following: more decentralized and flatter organizational structures; improved mangement information systems (MIS), which will become more responsive to line-management and user driven, while still geared to system-wide integration and the organization's diverse information needs (technical and data management); better mangement of transitions, not just change(transitions start with endings, not just new beginnings); the new technology will favor more experimental, small-scale projects, excellent for incremental learning and entrepreneurial risk taking; more mangers will become better conflict managers and also know how to communicate across traditional departmental or divisional boundaries; this will also require more participation by leaders in nonwork networks and in activities such as clubs, associations, charities, volunteer groups, lobbying efforts, community conflict negotiation etc.

The key task of organizational revitalization is the integration of people and business issues. Any human resource development plan should first include written objectives:

*To correlate the planning and implementation of human resource development efforts with the strategic needs of the entire organization.

*To decide what changes in organizational structure, management processes and personnel are required to achieve the objectives targeted in the strategic plan.

*To support an integrated plan for recruiting, selecting, promoting, compensating, and developing human resources, including executive succession.

Many questions arise that are relevant to our search for strategic revitalization and renewal. Some of the questions that will help us to explore these issues include:

1) How can we best identify the skills needed at each management or administrative level?

2) What steps can be taken in any functional area to prepare/identify people for special positions, like system integrator, organizational troubleshooter, ombudsperson, or roving M.B.W.A.(management by walking around) specialist?

3) How does our salary administration and benefits policy permit us to achieve our organizational objectives of obtaining and retaining qualified employees?

4) Which programs have been successful for implementing our various H.R. and business mission, goals, and objectives? Which have failed?

5) To what performance criteria should incentives be tied?

6) For what purposes should our appraisal programs be directed? Should they be tied to our stratgic direction and the type of employee we need as we face the 21s century?

7) What additional government controls/regulations do you see within the next five years? The next ten years? Are you prepared to fight them, encourage them, accept them at face value, or just react to them? Are you prepared to spend time, manpower, prestige, and money to achieve you goals and objectives in this area?

8) What do you see as the most significant factor(s)in our society tha will effect our ability to develop and market quality services and products at competitive prices?

9) What are our most effective current strategies, and how should we capitalize on them? What are most ineffective strategies and how can we convince others to abandon them?

10) What are our marginally vulnerable areas, and how can we improve in these areas?

Any program or effort for traing, education or skill improvement that impacts our revitalization and renewal efforts, must ultimately be implemented at the line management levels. Effective line management requires the utilization and assistance of proven human resource strategies and techniques. The reasons we mismanage employees is often because we lack of human resource knowledge or skills. Some of the reasons for this situation include:

1) *Limited understanding* of a more *flexible and participatory managerial philosophy*, which reduces employee motivation, trust and initiative.

2) *Limited time* spent with employees *communicating* about strategic mission, objectives, the business plan, how the reward system is designed to encourage more competive business behavior and quality, and why workers are an important part of the process.

3) The emphasis upon short-term payoffs and fad policies which ignore long-term human resources investment, and well thought-out, comprehensive strategies.

4) Poor education and training in managing and developing human resources--lack of knowledge regarding listening, interviewing, disciplining, delegating, compensating, and motivating.

5) Unrealistic and unclear standards about what job effectiveness quality means, which places unreasonable pressures on the employees to produce without the training and education to help them accomplish their goals. Quantity is often more important than quality.

6) Protectiveness and secrecy in personnel matters where line managers withhold important information regarding compensation policy and practice, standards for performance appraisal ratings, affirmative action plans, training and promotion opportunities. Feedback is essential for effective performance appraisal, trust, loyalty, and and a belief that salary compensation policies are fair.

7) The over emphasis upon formal personnel department staff for implementing human resource management policy. Personnel or human resource departments should primarily develop policy directives and support programs; practice and implementation of human resource policies should take place at the line or operational level, with the consultive assistance of human resouces.

REVITALIZING THE REWARD SYSTEM

Individuals join organizations and exchange their commitment and competence for extrinsic and intrinsic rewards. One of the more difficult tasks is assuring the adequacy of this exchange process. It is often easier to evaluate extrinsic rewards, because such rewards can be more readily defined and measured.   The more intangible, intrinsic rewards are more difficult to define and evaluate.

Problems arise when workers base their entire performance on the extrinisic rewards, like pay. Problems in work supervision, lack of career counseling and promotional opportunities are not compensation problems best handled by human resources profes- sional, but systems issue impacting the entire organization. Our pri- mary goal is then to understand how workers use the extrinsic reward system as focal point fo their dissatisfaction when the organization fails to provide any intrinsic rewards like involvement, participation and meaningful work.

Some human resource professionals believe that by increasing intrinsic rewards, the organization can lessen extrinsic compensation costs. In fact, the opposite may occur over the short-run, because those programs designed to increase intrinsic rewards, through more participative and innovative work systems, can be costly. Indirectly and over the longer-term, these intrinsic rewards can save money and increase productivity through work satisfaction, team effort, in- creased morale and motivation, higher quality work with fewer de- fects, and lower costs for turnover and absenteeism (Gutknecht and Miller, 1986; Gutknecht, 1985 and 1988).

The use of extrinsic rewards, like pay, can actually reduce the intrin- sic motivations that emerge from giving employee smore discretion and control over their work. By allowing management to manipulate (use as punishment) this powerful extrinisic reward, and making base-pay contingent upon poorly designed performance appraisal tools, intrinsic motivation can be undermined.

Intrinsic motivation is the opposite of dependency. Individuals set their own standards when their work is intrinsically important and enjoyable. Most negative feedback, like that used to punish poor performers in ineffectively designed pay-for-performance systems, can actually reduce intrinsic motivation. The strategic question is: how can we build a reward system that will work as an important motivation tool?

Rigidly designed, top-down, extrinsic reward systems, utilizing only the strategy of pay, can actually undermine the organization's strategic goals. Whatever you design make sure that it is communicating clearly and widely the benefits of both extrinsic reward policy, including pay and other benefits, and intrinsic issues like participation, recognition, trust and fairness. Motivation and effective performance are increased by employee beliefs that the organization is fair and responsive. Also, remember to let people know the dollar value of all their benefits in some form, like a hidden paycheck statement.

Several **action questions** that can help you to assess the reward system in your organization are listed below. What are the symbols of success in the organization? Does the organization provide an adequate mix of rewards, depending upon the people evaluated? Does the organization promote the misperception of how it rewards, because it fails to provide accurate information about salaries and the criteria for merit or performance? Does the organization raise expectations about the effectiveness of its pay-for-performance system, which falls far short in practice? Does the organization recognize that any well-designed pay system is built upon trust, good communication, clear standards, visibility, information, and fairness?

Does the organization recognize that pay-for-performance systems often end up rewarding ability and not effort, therefore requiring more investment in education, training, and employee development? Does the organization recognize that if employees participate in designing their reward system, particularly salary, their sense of trust, feelings of equity and general satisfaction will generally increase?

Compensation or reward systems should not be viewed primarily as a human resouces issue. Reward system policies should follow the strategic lead of organizational policies in all vital areas, including business plans, management philosophy and style, culture, employee involvement, training, career growth, structural and work design issues, among others. The dysfunctional and contradictory components of pay, and other extrinsic rewards that destroy intrinsic motivation, must be eliminated(see aso Gutknecht and Miller, 1986:269-284).

Compensation itself should not be used to punish workers; although wage levels can vary depending upon many factors, including inflation and performance. Using pay to punish deficient performance can actually create human resource problems. The reward system can, however, be used to reinforce desired organizational behaviors, attitudes and values.

The reward system should support other renewal policies. Money can be effectively used to motivate behavior, based upon flexible, fair and clearly communicated standards for performance. However, the compensation system must interact with other organizational and external conditions, like labor markets or competition, to determine effective and productive performance. A better system is to provide more diverse rewards and numerous opportunities for work satisfaction.

STRATEGIC REVITALIZATION FOR TOMORROW'S ORGANIZATION

Organizations that are positioning themselves for future opportunities must anticipate the changing trends and threats in a competitive world. In this sections, we will review some of the important trends that suggests ways for human resources to assist the organization to maintain its strategic direction.

GAIN SHARING AND PROFIT SHARING

Gain-sharing and profit sharing plans are seen increasing in many progressive organizations. The gain-sharing plan, like the Scalon plan, tries to match pay with the overall performance of a unit larger than the individual. A bonus can be shared by individuals in the department or entire organization, based upon some measureable improvement, in the use of cash, labor, materials, supplies that results in improved productivity, profits, or sales.

The gain-sharing formula must include the following three components: 1) participative administration in the design, maintenance and execution of the plan; 2) performance must be measured beyond the individual employee level; 3) the organizational culture and leadership must communicate the benefits of increased cooperation and teamwork. The fact that gains are tied to increased work productivity (which discounts possibilities of favoritism), and the reduced administrative overload of constantly doing performance evaluation(not eliminated), saves money and reduces negative feedback, which can destroy motivation.

Profit sharing and stock ownership plans are less effective than pay-for-performance programs as motivators of performance, because the link between individual performance and corporate performance (via stock or sharing profits) in large organizations is difficult to establish. The value of such systems resides in their symbolic and motivational aspects. Organizations are saying that we are a team, and we are all owners together, and each of us is an important part of this total, long-term effort to improve our productivity.

Often the best compensation systems include some combination of individual pay-for-performance and gain-sharing components. In addition, as we've already discussed, any compensation system should try to align itself with other systems to encourage participation, team-work, quality, involvement, innovation, self-management, job enrichment, management development and employee training. Any integrated program for renewal must link financial, psychological, and security incentives.

PAY AS A MANAGEMENT TOOL

No matter what kind of pay system an organization utilizes, it is the manager in charge who decides whether an emploee gets a raise and for how much. The *Sweedish Employers Confederation* notes that a given organizational pay classificaion system may cut across diverse jobs whose content and skill requirements greatly differ. Thus, managers need better guidelines in order to adapt a pay system to particular organizational needs.

A primary dimension is that the time on the job does not indicate merit, unless performance is is measured. Senority may give an employee greater knowledge, experience, responsibility, versatility, maturity and the the ablity to produce desired results. Therefore, any system that relies upon the evaluation of skills and expertise in performance recognition should also recognize the assets that productive senority brings.

Here then are some more **action suggestions** for your consideration. Set up a pay system to also reward in some degree the factors listed below. The relative importance of each factor depends upon the particular industry, organization and job. Standards for each job might be set up using each dimension to yield accurate comparisions across classifications. Measure whether each worker falls short, meets or exceeds the standard.

* Reward **results** on the job, whether individually or team-based, because they provide a solid yardstick about each employee's contribution to the company.

* **Knowledge** of the job or **information** about how the job most effectively works is an important componet. This information can help establish its financial value by identifying the costs of recruiting and training the replacement position.

* **Responsibility** for key delivery dates, product introduction deadlines, upgrading of old products or plans, quality, use of highly technical equipment and numerous other important industry parameters can also become important.

* Reward **versatility** because the modern organization improves its productivity when it can flexibly assign workers a wide variety of tasks, or promote talent and find that they have not reached their level of incompetence.

FUTURE INNOVATIONS FOR A MORE PROACTIVE HR

Trends and innovations on the horizon in progressive organizations:

HR curriculums will shift from just functional to include behavioral and cognitive skills and will introduce new teaching methods, 'hands on' projects, more innovative simulations, cooperative education, more computer applications, internships and work experience.

Non-cognitive skills will also gain credibility within HR students and negotiating skills will have to be enhanced.

There will be greater emphasis on ethics, morals and the process of action and active learning, as well as, on the quality of the inputs and process dimensions, not just outputs.

HR will increasingly utilize its roots in interdisciplinary studies to learn even more about foreign cultures, values, language, customs and business practices internationally. The dominant intellectual bias toward the west will slowly shift toward understanding more about cultures in the Pacific-Asian Rim and South American neighbors.

HR will support a greater exercise of creativity, flexibility, openness, and democracy in modern organizations.

A sample of creative possibilities in the areas of recruitment, selection, training, monitoring, counseling and evaluation, include the following:

The use of video tapes or discs to show the advantages of working in a particular company and the submission of video data about the capabilities of candidates to employers.

Use of video documents for preliminary interviews of candidates, and live satelite television interviews of prospects from all over the world. Here media and computer literacy will assist the

HR professionals to gain a career edge in using advanced communication technology, such as CD ROM technology for educational transmission around the world or for use in on-line customized data bases.

The use of simulation techniques for both computer and gaming procedures, will improve the quality of assessment centers, for both new hires and promotion of current personnel. These and other methods will expand the focus on the need for more managers and workers with improved intercultural communication abilities, abstract thinking capability, the ability to synthesize large amounts of information, and display advanced technological and informational competencies.

Employment and evaluation of group-orientated problem-solving methods by using video tapes, case-studies, dramatized critical incident, and technological forecasts will be more common.

Organizational learning centers will be electronically connected with the employee's home communication system or with university educational services.

Special simulated preparations for reaching unusual relocations or recruiting for nontraditional careers, similar to the type of orientation and training given to the astronauts for their space activities and moon walk, will ocur more frequently.

Content of training courses will be based on future studies, trends, issues management strategies, technological forecasts, as well as global, and interplanetary data bases and around the clock on line uses of information.

Improved search-and-support strategies to recruit top-performing, nonconforming, and exceptional workers (organizational scanners and innovators) will increase. These individuals will then be utilized as problem solvers, conflict managers, ombudsperson, exemplary spokespeople, organizational troubleshooters, and behavioral models.

Integration and use of people differences and diversity (in terms of their capabilities, handicaps, culture, education, experience or aspiration) will increase so that each employee's unique needs are recognized in the design of facilities, provisions for career development or accomodations of job requirements.

Use of a variety of techniques to provide personal and professional growth, ranging from career exchanges and educational sabbaticals to new compensation benefits and personnel services.

References

Abernathy, William, K. Clark, and A. Kantrow.

1983   **Industrial Renaissance: Producing a Competitive Future for America**. New York: Basic Books.

Ackoff, Russell L.

1981   **Creating the Corporate Future**. New York: John Wiley & Sons.

Adams, J.

1974   **Conceptual Blockbusting**. Stanford, CA: The Portable Stanford.

Albert, Michael and Murray Silverman.

1984   *Making Management Philosophy a Cultural Reality, Part 1: Get Started*. **Personnel**. Jan.-Feb.: 12-21.

Aldrich H. E. and J. Pfeffer.

1976   *"Environments and Organizations."* **Annual Review of Sociology**, No. 2: 79-105.

Allen, Robert F.
   1984   **Lifegain**. New York: Appleton-Century-Crofts.

Bales, R.R.
   1950   **Interaction Process Analysis: A Method for The Study of Groups.** Reading Mass.: Addison-Wesley.

Bennis, Warren and Burt Nanus.
   1985   **Leaders: Strategies For Taking Charge.** New York: Harper and Row.

Bennis, Warren.
1983 *"The Art Form of Leadership."* **The Executive Mind.** San Francisco, CA: Jossey-Bass, Inc.

Benson, Herbert. **The Relaxation Response.** New York: Avon Books,1975.

Bion, W.R.
   1961 **Experiences in Groups.** London: Tavistock.

Bisesi, Michael.
   1983   *"Strategies for Successful Leadership in Changing Times."* **Sloan Management Review.** Fall: 61-64.

Brym, J.

1980 **Intellectuals and Politics.** London: George Allen and Unwin.

Burke, W. Warner.

1982 **Organization Development: Principles and Practices.** Englewood Cliffs, NJ: Prentice-Hall.

Burns, J.

1978 **Leadership.** New York: Harper and Row.

Buzan, Tony.

1974 **Using Both Sides of Your Brain.** New York: E.P. Dutton Inc.

Chalofsky, Neal and Carnie Ives Lincoln.

1983 **Up the HRD Ladder: A Guide for Professional Growth.** Reading, MA: Addison-Wesley.

Churchman, C.W.

1979 **The Systems Approach and Its Enemies.** New York: Basic Books.

Cohen, Alan. S. Fink, H. Gaddon, and R. Willits.

1980 **Effective Behavior in Organizations.** Homewood,

Ill.: Richard D. Irwin.

Crawford, R.

1954   **Techniques of Creative Thinking**. New York:
Hawthorn Books, Inc.

Crozier, Michael and E. Friedberg.

1980   **Actors and Systems: The Politics of Collective
Action.**   Chicago, IL: University of Chicago Press.

Deal, Terrence E. and Allan A. Kennedy.

1982   **Corporate Cultures: The Rites and Rituals of
Corporate Life.** Reading, MA: Addison-Wesley.

DeBono, E.

1967   **The Uses of Lateral Thinking**. New York: Basic
Books.

Deci, E.L.

1973   *"Paying People Doesn't Always Work the Way You Expect
It To*." **Human Resource Management**. Vol. 12, Summer: 28-32.

Dewey, John.

1933   **How We Think**. Lexingon, MA: D.C. Heath.

Drucker, Peter.

  1985   **Innovation and Entrepreneurship.** New York:
Harper & Row.

Deming, W. Edwards.

  1988   **Roadmap For Change: The Deming Approach.** New
York: Encyclopaedia Britannica Educational Corporation.

Dunn, Halbert L.

   1961.   **High Level Wellness.** Arlington, Va.: R.W. Beatty.

Ellis, Albert and Robert Harper.

  1979   **A Guide to Rational Living.** Englewood Cliffs, N.J.:
Prentice Hall.

Farrel, L.

  1986   *"Building Entrepreneurship: A Global Perspective."*
Training Magazine. Vol 23: 422-550.

Ferguson, Marilyn.

  1980   **The Aquarian Conspiracy: Personal and Social
Transformation in the 1980's.** Los Angeles: J.P. Tarcher.

Fiedler, F.E.

  1974   *"The Contingency Model: New Directions for Leadership*

Utilization." **Journal of Contemporary Business.** Autumn, 3 (4): 65-80.

1967   "The Contingency Model: New Directions for Leadership." **Utilization. Journal of Contemporary Business.** Autumn, 3 (4): 65-80.

Friedman, Meyer and Diane Ulme.r
    1984   **Treating Type A Behavior and Your Heart.** New York: Alfred A. Knopf.

Girdano, Daniel and George Everly.
    1986   **Controlling Stress and Tension: A Holistic Approach.** Englewood Cliffs, N.J.: Prentice Hall.

Frost, Peter
    1984   *"Blind Spots in the Study of Organizations: Some Implementa-tions for Teaching and Application"*. In Douglas B. Gutknecht (Ed.). **Meeting Organization and Human Resource Challenges: Perspectives, Issues and Stategies.** Lanham, MD: University Press of America

Gutknecht, Douglas and Janet Miller.
    1986   **The Organizational and Human Resources Sourcebook.** Lanham, MD: University Press of America.

Gutknecht, Douglas B.

   1988   **Designing Health Promotion Systems: Strategies For Individual Wellness and Organizational Health.** Los Angeles, Ca.: Human Resources Press.

   1985   **Strategic Revitalization: People, Processes and Systems.** Lanham, Maryland: University Press of America.

   1982   *"Sociobiology."* **Free Inquiry in Creative Sociology.** Vol 5. No 1.

   1981   *"Sociobiology: The Debate Continues."* **Western Sociological Review.** Vol 2, No. 3.

J. Hackman, J.R. and G.R. Oldham.

   1980   **Work Redesign.** Reading, MA: Addison-Wesley.

Herzberg, Mausner B. and B. Syderman.

   1959   **The Motivation to Work.** New York: John Wiley and Sons.

Hickman, Craig R. and Michael A. Silva.

   1984   **Creating Excellence: Managing Corporate Culture, Strategy and Change in a New Age.** New York: New American Library.

House, J.R.

1971 *"A Path-Goal Theory of Leader Effectivenss."*
Administrative Science Quarterly. 16: 321-339.

House, J.R. and G. Dessler.

1974 *"The path-Goal Theory of Leadership: Some Post-Hoc and
A Priori Tests. J. Hunt and L. Larson."* (eds.). **Contingency
Approaches to Leadership.** Carbondale, IL: Southern Illinois
University Press.

Janis, Irvin.

1982 **Group Think.** 2d. ed. Boston: HoughtonMifflin.

Johnston, Joseph S. and Associates.

1986 **Educating Managers: Executive Effectiveness
Through Liberal Learning.** San Francisco, Ca.: Jossey-Bass
Publishers.

Jones, Landon.

1980 **Great Expectations: American and the Baby Boom
Generation.** New York: Vintage Press.

Kanter, Rosabeth Moss.

1983 **The Change Masters: Innovation for Productivity
in the American Corporation.** New York: Simon and Shuster.

Kellerman, Barbara.

1984   **Leadership: Interdisciplinary Perspectives.** New York: Prentice-Hall.

Kerr, Clarke.

1973   *"Introduction: Industrialism With a Human Face."* In Clark Kerr (ed.). **Work in America: The Decade Ahead.** New York: Van Nostrand Reinhold.

Kirkpatrick, Donald L.

1988   **How To Manage Change Effectively.** San Francisco, Ca.: Jossey-Bass, Inc.

Knight, D. and J. Roberts.

1982   *"The Power of Organization or the Organization of Power."* **Organization Studies.** Vol. 5, No.1: 47-633.

Latham, Gary P. and Edwin A. Locke.

1979   *"Goal Setting--A Motivational Technique That Works."* **Organizational Dynamics.** Autumn, 68-74.

Lazarus, Richard S.

1984   " Puzzles in the Study of Daily Hassles." **Journal of Behavioral Medicine**, No. 7: 375-389.

Lewin, Kurt.

1946   *"Action Research and Minority Problems."* **Journal of Social Issues.** 2: 148-163.

Likert, Rensis.

1961   **New Patterns of Management.** New York: McGraw-Hill.

Lukes, Steven.

1976   **Power: A Radical View.**   New York: MacMillan.

Lundbert, Craig C.

1969   *"On the Usefulness of Organizational Rascals."* **The Business Quarterly.** Winter.

Lynch, D.

1984   **Your High-Performance Business Brain: An Operator's Manual.** New York: Prentice-Hall.

McCall, T. and P.Zimbardo.

1983   *"Reasons Leaders Fail."* **Psychology Today.**

Maier, Norman R.F.

1970   **Problem Solving and Creativity in Individuals and Groups.** Monterey, CA: Brooks/Cole.

Maslow, A.H.

1970   **Motivation and Personality.** (Rev. ed.). New York: Harper & Row.

1965   **Euspsychian Management: Making Good Management Better.** Homewood, IL: Richard D. Irwin Inc. and The Dorsey Press.

Matherly, T. and R. Goldsmith.

1987   *"The Two Faces of Creativity."* **Business Horizons.** Vol. 28: 8-11.

Mayo, Elton.

1939   *"Routine Interaction and the Problems of Collaboration."* **American Sociological Review.** 4: 335-340.

McClellan, D.

1961   **The Achieving Society.** Princeton, NJ: Van Nostrand Reinhold.

McGregor, D.

1960   **The Human Side of Enterprise.** New York: McGraw-Hill.

Moberg, S.

   1984   **Organizational Health Promotion Evaluation.** New
York: Prtentice Hall.

Naisbitt, J.

   1982   **Megatrends.** New York: Warner.

Odiorne, George S.

   1981   **The Change Resistors.** Englewood Cliffs, NJ: Spectrum
Books.

   1984   **Strategic Management of Human Resources.** San
Francisco, Ca.: Jossey-Bass.

Oldham, G. R.

   1976   *"Job Characteristics and Internal Motivation: The
Moderation Effect of Interpersonal and Individual Variables."*.
Human Relations. 29: 550-569.

Opatz, Joseph.
   1985   **A Primer of Health Promotion: Creating Healthy
Organizational Cultures.** Washington D. C.: Oryn Publishing Co.

Osborn, A.

   1963   **Applied Imagination** (3rd ed.). New York: Scribner.

Ouchi, William G.

   1981   **Theory Z: How American Business Can meet the Japanese Challenge.** Reading, MA: Addison-Wesley.

Paton, Michael Quinn.

   1987   **Creative Evaluation.** 2nd. Ed. Beverly Hills, Ca.; Sage Publications.

Pelletier, Kennth R.

   1984 **Healthy People in Unhealthy Places: Stress and Fitness at Work.** New York: Delacorte Press.

Perkins, A.

   1981 **The Mind's Best Work.** Boston, MA: Harvard University Press.

Peters, T.H. and R.J. Waterman.

   1982 **In Search of Excellence: Lessons From America's Best Run Companies.** New York: Harper & Row.

Pfeffer, Jeffrey.

   1981   *"Management as Symbolic Action: The Creation and Maintenance of Organizational Paradigms"*. R. Cummings (ed.). **Research in Organizational Behavior.** Vol 3. New york: Jai Press.

Porter, L.W. and E.E. Lawler, III.

1968 **Managerial Attitudes and Performance.** Homewood, IL: Irwin.

Reich, Robert B.

1983   **The Next American Frontier.** New York: Harper & Row.

Robbins, Stephen

1983   **Organizational Behavior.** New York: Prentice Hall.

Salancik, G. R. and J. Pfeffer.

1977   *"An Examination of Needs-Satisfaction Models of Job Satisfaction."* **Administrative Science Quarterly.** Vol. 23, No. 2: 225-253.

Scherer, Greg.
  1983.   **Information Packet of Scherer Lumber Company Program.**

Schon, Donald A.

1983   **The Reflective Practitioner: How Professionals Think in Action.** New York: Basic Books.

Schuster, J.

1984   *"Whole-Brain Training: Ticket To The Information Age"?*

Training Magazine. April: 52-59.

Schuster, Frederic E.

   1986   **Schuster Report: The Proven Connection between People and Profits**. New York: John Wiley and Son.

Seyle, Hans.

   1976   **The Stress of Life**. New York: McGraw Hill.

   1974.   **Stress Without Distress**. New York: New American Library.

Sinetar, M.

   1985   *"Entrepreneurs, Chaos, and Creativity--Can Creative People Really Survive Large Company Cultures"?* **Sloan Management Review**. Vol. 26: 57-611.

Smirchich, Linda.

   1983   *"Studying Organizations as Cultures."* **Beyond Method: Strategies for Social Research**. Beverly Hills, CA: Sage Publications, Inc.

Taylor, F.

   1967   **The Principles of Scientific Management**. New York: Norton.

Van Maanen and Edgar Schein.

1978   *"Toward a Theory of Organizational Socialization."* In Barry Staw (ed.). **Annual Review of Research in Organizational Behavior.** New York: Jai Press.

Vickers, Sir Geoffrey.

1984   **Human Systems Are Different.** New York: Harper & Row.

Weber, Max.

1946 **From Max Weber, Essays in Sociology.** Trans. and Ed. by Hans Gerth and C. Wright Mills. New York: Oxford University.

Weick, Karl.

1979 **The Social Psychology of Organizing** (2nd ed.). Reading, MA: Addison-Wesley.

Wissema, J.G., H.W. Vander Pol, and H.M. Messer.

1980   *"Strategic Management Archetypes."* **Strategic Management Journal.** Vol. 43.

Yankelovich, Daniel.

1981 **New Rules: Searching for Fulfillment in a World Turned Upside Down.** New York: Vintage Books.

Waterman, Robert H.

  1988   **The Renewal Factor: How The Best Companies Get and Keep The Competitive Edge.** New York: Bantam Books.

  Yavitz, Boris.

  1988   *" Human Resources in Strategic Planning."* In Ginzberg (Eds.) **Executive Talent: Developing and Keeping the Best People.** New York: John Wiley & Sons.

Weitzen, H. Skip.

  1988   **Infopreneurs: Turning Data Into Dollars.** New York: John Wiley & Sons.

Ziegenfuss, A.

  1988   **Organizational Troubleshooters.** San Francisco, Ca.: Jossey-Bass Inc.

Zierden, A.

  1980   *" Leading From the Followers Point of View."* **Organizational Dynamics.** Vol. 3.